Dear Dr. ...

Thank you for

such an inspiration.

Peace, love & Pears!

Christina Porter

Praise for Christine Porter

"After 30 years as a hospice nurse, I have heard many end of life reviews by individuals facing a terminal illness. The questions posed in this book bear a startling resemblance to the musings of those facing the end of their life. What a gift to address these core human issues while there is still a lifetime of opportunity for change or reconciliation."

- Catherine Esterheld BSN. MS
Retired Director of Palliative Care Concepts, Inc.

"I absolutely love this book. I found her voice refreshing filled with spiritual ideas and principles mixed with stories of her own personal journey. It's like sitting down with a dear friend and having a heartfelt conversation where she shares words of wisdom with me. I loved this book."

- Tracy Blair
Awakened Soul Yoga and Poet

"The Wisdom of You was a true gift, and it came to me at a time when I needed it most. Christine's writing is genuine, insightful and honest. I can't wait to pass along this gift to the people I love. An absolute must-read."

- Nicole Sheldon
Reporter at RBJ/BridgeTower Media and Blogger

THE WISDOM OF YOU

A TRANSFORMATIONAL JOURNEY
TO CREATING AN EXTRAORDINARY LIFE

Christine Porter

Softcover ISBN: 978-1-7330686-0-4

1st edition, May 2019
Printed in the United States of America

This book is dedicated to some very special people in my life. To my mother, for her unwavering encouragement, sound advice and incredible strength and love she has shared with me through the years.

My dear soul sisters Tracy and Lili, who have always been by my side cheering me on and supporting me on this crazy journey of life. You are the family I always wanted and needed and I love you both! Each one of you is a Soulful Warrior making the world a better place.

Contents

Introduction

*Life transformation can happen at any age
and at any time. It can be blissfully exciting,
empowering and fun!*

Why did I write this book? To help folks slow down
and reconnect with themselves and those they care about.
To find a simpler, healthier life full of passion and purpose.
I believe that every single one of us is here on this earth
for a reason. It's our life's work to figure out who we really
are, what we think, what we feel and what our unique gifts
are, so we can make a difference in our world. It's possible
for each of us to create a meaningful life where we feel
energized, fulfilled, happy and raise others up with us. It's
also possible to release so much of the fear and anxiety that
plagues our minds and bodies, causing us to miss sleep, feel
chronically depleted, moody, and often leading to aches
and pains and chronic illnesses. Our bodies are constantly
giving us messages that it's time to pay attention to our
lifestyle and our mindset. They are a barometer for what is
happening in our subconscious. It can start out fairly simple:
a lower back pain that lasts for a few days or maybe weeks,
persistent headaches, tightness in the chest or an upset
stomach. What's causing these pains? Is it too much
sitting and working long hours without enough breaks?
Is it the stress and anxiety of our work or home life? Are

we eating on the run all the time and putting poor-quality foods in our bodies? Is it the feeling of never having enough and needing to achieve more? For many of us it can just be the malaise of a routine that no longer serves us.

The good news is that at any point in time, you can change your life and feel better. There isn't any magic bullet, but the tools I would like to share with you are free and accessible to everyone. They have been studied by neuroscientists, physicians, philosophers, spiritualists, yogis and clergy. These practices can have life-changing impact and only require a little time, energy and the curiosity to explore the wisdom that lies within you. Once you slow down and reconnect with yourself, you will begin to feel a shift.

It is my hope that the products I've created, the books I write and the workshops and retreats I facilitate will help you connect to your own inner guidance to help you understand the path toward what's most meaningful for you. It is also my hope that I can help guide you in finding balance in your life, and as a result, more happiness and fulfillment. This is your one and only life at this moment; how will you show up for it today?

How did I find my path? It wasn't so long ago I was in career burnout, facing a mid-life crisis, searching for who I was and how to feel better. I was going through a painful breakup, suffering great betrayal from someone I loved deeply. My five-year journey was challenging, and I struggled to find meaning and purpose. I wondered where my unique journey would lead me and how quickly I could get through all the pain and discomfort. I wanted the shortcut to my happiness plan. When that didn't come, I decided to try anything and everything I could find to feel and think better. That's when I made a commitment to try meditation and revive my journaling practice. I began reading about a variety of mindfulness and spiritual practices. I dug through my health coaching toolkit and began using the tools I used on my coaching clients on myself. I attended online and in-person workshops, went on yoga and meditation retreats, changed my eating patterns again. I spent more time in nature and reconnected with friends that were once so important to me. I bet my journey isn't as unique as I might have thought at one time.

> *"We see our world through the lens of our own unique perspective."*
> – Christine Porter

We are all unique people having a human experience. Each one of us responds to stress, excitement, disappointment, approval, advancement, family, diet, exercise, love and our environment differently. This is what makes each of us individual. Yet most of us have a longing to feel connected and accepted, to be loved and protected. We make the best choices we know at that time to get our wants and needs fulfilled. Sometimes they work in our favor; other times they fall flat and we're left wondering "why me?" and "how'd I get here?"

What happens when these choices don't work out for our best interests? How we react is just as important as how we think. During my dark period I had to ask myself:

Am I a victim in this game of life or a co-creator? Do I blame others for the events and feelings I'm experiencing or do I realize my actions have led me to this place? Is there a larger force guiding me in another direction for my highest good, even when I can't see it right away? Am I able to sit still, contemplate the lessons and go deep within for the right next move? Is gratitude a part of my daily thoughts or am I rushing by so quickly I barely see the stop signs, let alone finding the joy in the little gifts of the day? Have I been burying my feelings and acting out with food or alcohol to numb the frustration, sadness, loneliness or feelings of helplessness? Can I sit with myself alone, quietly and ask myself what I'm really craving? Are you up for the challenge?

How am I showing up for my life, right here, right now? That question kept coming back to me. My corporate job taught me how resilient, tenacious and fearless I am. I acquired new skills, honed my talents and learned the masterful art of negotiation. I also learned that I like to help people and solve problems. This became a character defect that led me to taking on everyone's tough projects at work and trying to fix what really couldn't be fixed alone. It required motivation and teamwork, something our department lacked. I overstepped my bounds more times than not and tried to tackle everyone's problems. This wasn't good for me or them. I became exhausted, depleted and resentful of having to carry the whole load. I was robbing people of the opportunity to work it out themselves, to speak up for themselves to honor and develop their own skills. Lesson learned.

My marriage taught me what it feels like to truly be vulnerable, to trust and love deeply. It didn't work out the way I wanted it to. In one fateful day, I felt like a wrecking ball went through my life. It was a painful time, but it taught me so many valuable lessons and sent me on a path of self-exploration and spiritual development that I might not have come to otherwise. For that I'm grateful.

I didn't become the victim in either life situation. Sure, there were times I cried for hours, even days, and sometimes I just felt hopeless. I allowed myself to feel these tough feelings but I didn't stay in that place for long and I vowed to not let it define me or break me.

I want to share the techniques I used to create a better life through a better way of thinking. You may not be going through a major life crisis. You may be content in your life at this very moment. But what if I told you there were some simple techniques you could learn to help you live a less stressful life, sleep better, lose some weight, communicate more effectively, learn to appreciate the little things and help become a catalyst for change in your own life and your community?

The body and mind connection is powerful but still often overlooked, even in today's medical society. What if I told you there was a way to a healthier life, a healthier body—and it wasn't just about starting another diet? Most of us focus on our family's genes and anticipate we may also suffer from our ancestors' illnesses. After all, we've been told "it's hereditary." While that might be true, there is another version of the story worth exploring. Epigenetics is the study of biological mechanisms that will switch genes on and off. Epigenetics is everywhere: what we eat, where we live, who we interact with, when we sleep, how we exercise, even aging—all of these can eventually cause chemical modifications around the genes that will turn those genes on or off over time.

As bestselling author Christiane Northrup, M.D., explains, your destiny is not entirely defined by your genes. We are learning that your genes cause less than 10 percent of all diseases. So, if your genes aren't driving disease, what is?

According to Northrup, epigenetics, the study of how our environment affects our genes, is far more accurate in determining our health. We know that eating nutritious foods, being physically active doing things you love, and making other smart, healthy lifestyle choices to reduce your stress level, can improve your health. It's also important to pay attention to your beliefs. Your beliefs, along with your relationships, the way you handle stress, the foods you eat are all factors that contribute to how your genes are expressed.

This is how important the body and mind connection is. It's not just a new-age way to look at life; there is scientific evidence, as explained by neuroscientists, that our thoughts and feelings play a role in our health and our life success. Think about all the ways we sidetrack ourselves or keep ourselves stuck. Often times, we don't even recognize we are being self-destructive. Many of our thoughts and how we see the world are habits we created from the time we were very young. It's how we learned to interpret our world and how to keep ourselves feeling safe and in control.

But is it serving us well as adults? Are those thoughts, worries and negative feelings helping us to reach our highest potential and feel good?

According to Joe Dispenza, D.C., a leading neuro-scientist, bestselling author and researcher in the fields of neuroscience, epigenetics and quantum physics, you have the ability to train your brain to improve your health and well-being and create the life you want. "Each time you make a new choice that is in alignment with your future, you are priming your brain to install the neurological hardware to actually think, act and feel like the person you want to be in your future."

In my workshops, I teach five things that you need to quit to catalyze positive change in your life:

- fearing change
- trying to please everyone
- overthinking and obsessing
- living in the past and putting too much focus on the future
- and criticizing yourself and others, or falling into the "judgement trap"

It's important for us to learn to quiet our minds and decrease our stress levels, find balance and purpose and foster deeper connections with ourselves and the ones we care about in order for us to be happier and healthier. How can we do this when we are so pressured and short of time? The techniques in this book are easy to incorporate into your daily life and are meant to be done just a few minutes each day.

The number one rule I began to understand and the

most important tool I share in this book is to stop looking outside of yourself for the answers. Your power lies in going within, connecting with yourself on a deeper level than maybe you ever have. Everything you need to know is deep inside of you if you just learn how to tap into this inner guidance, or call it your intuition. It is your internal GPS system; we all have one.

"Everything you need to know is inside of you.
Every question, every answer, and every right move.
It's an inside job."

– Christine Porter

Some key thoughts to explore on your journey:

- You don't have to take life as it comes. This is your one and only life at this moment and you don't want to be sitting on the sidelines letting everything happen to you. So, what is it going to be? You get to decide, every day. Starting today, you can make the next chapter of your life exciting, rewarding, fulfilling, productive and amazing. Feel the energy in your thoughts and aspirations and let the momentum move you.

- The purpose of this book is to inspire you and get you to slow down, go within, find your balance and let your imagination flow. Ask yourself; What will my life look like five or ten years from now? What do I really want to do? Where do I really want to go? The goal is not to create a list of "shoulds" but to stir up some exciting possibilities of what "could" be done in your one and only beautiful life. You get to decide, right here, right now.

At the end of some of the chapters there is a notes section with powerful questions to help prompt your transformation. Some of the other chapters feature 30-Day Challenges. I created these challenges initially for myself before I ever wrote this book. I was desperate to make some real, sustainable changes that would help me create a new life I could find fulfilling and peaceful. I knew I would have to change. I couldn't think and act the same way all my life and expect big changes. I wanted to explore new ideas, thoughts and patterns I could stick with to transform my life. I took a chance, stuck with it for 30 days and they became habits that I was enjoying. I saw results. I began using them in my workshops to provide practical ways participants could explore and find their own path long after the workshops were over.

I encourage you to try each of the 30-Day Challenges and explore for yourself. Set the pace for yourself and know these challenges are not designed to be used in any particular order. You may choose to try one or more at any given time. Some may stick for a lifetime, some may wax and wane. One thing I can promise you for sure: they will get you exploring your world in a different way. If you stick with it, you will be happier, calmer, more self-assured and on the path to creating your best life yet.

What I do as a coach, a workshop and retreat facilitator, speaker and author is to teach people how to become the best version of themselves; happy, healthy and fulfilled. It's that simple. This book outlines ten tools that will help you get in touch with the Wisdom of You and begin to lead your best life yet. Now let's begin this journey together.

Chapter 1:
Finding the Soulful Warrior Within

....

Inside all of us there is a strength and wisdom that knows what is best for us. It sometimes takes a life crisis or deep pain to slow us down before we can learn how to access it. Once you start on the journey, you can begin to feel a sense of peace with this new awareness. It can be addictive, in a good way. The outcome is really about finding out who you truly are when you strip away the titles, your occupation, your family status and all the frills that give you a sense of identity.

I created my first product, Soulful Connections, as I began my own journey into self-discovery. I found that I was asking myself some big life questions that I had never really stopped to think about in the past. Which of my personal beliefs was preventing me from making the changes I needed to make in my life? What would I most love to do if I wasn't afraid of failure? What are my greatest talents? Do I believe everything in my life is happening for a reason, or are they just coincidences? Where do I want to be a year or five years from now?

At the time, I was very self-involved in furthering my career and was content to live on autopilot. Actually, I didn't even realize that's what I was doing until I hit the proverbial wall and my life began falling apart. I remember tearing up and feeling a great sense of despair almost every day as I walked into my office building. I struggled with my feelings and tried to push them aside. I was chasing the money, not my dreams.

I became so overwhelmed by the workload, managing unhappy people in a cutthroat work culture. I felt like I was losing myself, and I became increasingly depressed. I had left my freelance business I held for over a decade to take this job that landed in my lap, and I began feeling guilty for even thinking about leaving. It was a dream job on paper, but I knew, on some level, it wasn't where I needed or wanted to be. I had been enticed by the job offer to join the management team. This corporate job offered me the financial security I didn't have in my freelance business as the recession grew in my home city. I also knew that if I stayed at this job I would be miserable, sick and unhealthy. When I looked around at my coworkers, I could see the sadness and frustration they shared as well. There was an epidemic of powerlessness happening that no one was willing to recognize.

I stayed in the job far too long because I was scared. I kept rethinking the same scenarios over in my head. Where would I go? How would I restart my freelance business? How would I afford to live? Could I go to work for someone else again? What if the bigger problem was I wasn't enjoying my career anymore and was struggling to find what would make me happy? I was stuck in my own story. I became immobilized with growing feelings of self-doubt and inadequacy. That's what happens when you are working and living in a culture of negativity. It is systemic and fuels up on people's fears, their growing animosity of not being heard, not being challenged enough, and feeling overwhelmed and undervalued.

"What you resist, persists."
– Carl Jung

When we give away our power and let fear take control, a part of us slowly dies. Even when we make a commitment to ourselves to find the silver lining, to try and make the best of a bad situation, we are creating resistance. Resistance is the reason we stay stuck in patterns that keep us from thriving.

We tell ourselves all kinds of stories to try and make our less-than-desirable situation feel okay. Maybe we are feeling lazy and the strategy of ignoring what is painful or boring works for a while. You may say things like, "That's just the way I am," or, "I have plenty of reasons to be angry," and "This is just the way it is." You may be haunted by self-doubt and feelings of inadequacy so you condone your behavior and continue on.

We tend to carry an unconscious belief that in order to stay alive, we must hold on to our protection mechanism. We give our pain purpose and believe that the struggle is real. We begin to believe we must master life in order to feel safe and acquire success.

I decided it was time for me to take a long, hard look at my life, what I had created, the stories I was telling myself and decide if I wanted to continue on this path. Was I happy with the walls I had built for my illusion of safety and happiness? Was it time to shift directions and create a new freedom for myself that would require me to let go of my fears and resistance to life? What was my big dream for my life? If I knew I only had a few months to live, would I have regrets for not following my heart? I was feeling so scattered, keeping myself stuck in the daily grind, that I didn't have the answers to any of these questions. I was so busy living in survival mode that one day turned into the next.

That's where the plot twist in my life came in. I decided to start meditating. I initially sat quietly, thinking it might help me slow down and relax. I was overstimulated at work all day. There was always a steady parade of people needing my attention filtering in and out of my office, endless meetings and unrealistic deadlines. I was burned out and exhausted. But nothing could have prepared me for what came next.

That same year, struggling with my new job, I found out my husband was leading a double life. It happened by chance, and within a matter of a few minutes, I learned about the lies, deception and betrayal. I uncovered the ugly truth that I was not living with the person I thought I was. The pain was overwhelming. I now know what it feels like to be sucker punched. I couldn't catch my breath. There were moments when I thought it was just a bad dream, not being able to wrap my head around what was happening. I felt guilt and shame that I didn't see the warning signs or worse, chose to ignore them. I struggled with loving someone so much but also feeling so angry I could feel my blood pressure in my head as if it would explode. I lived with these feelings for a long time as I sat with my pain. I had lost myself; my life didn't feel like my own anymore, and a quiet desperation set in. I tried to pretend everything would be okay just so I could get up and go to work each day. I would panic most days that I would not be able to function because I was so distracted, scared and in pain. I worried I would lose control and that frightened me at a core level.

The following weeks and months I pulled the mask away and began the slow climb out of my own fantasy land. I was left with cognitive dissonance – trying to resolve in my mind how he could be so good and yet do really bad things behind my back. There was no outward abuse. He acted kind, gentle, empathetic, was highly educated and respected by his peers. He was everything I had looked for in a partner. None of that matters when you realize the past several years had been filled with lies, emotional abandonment, unnecessary drama for distraction, and a massive dose of denial on my part in an effort to keep the illusion of the family together.

I knew my life would never be the same, and I made the decision to leave my job and my husband. I wanted to be happy again. I wanted to feel healthy and not feel so anxious. I wanted to be able to sleep again; to feel a sense of safety and maybe a little peace. That was all I thought I needed at that time.

As I began meditating, I was asking for guidance. I wanted to get in touch with that quiet space inside of me that would be a barometer for how I was feeling. Maybe shed some light on what my next move should be. It was at that point I realized I needed to make some big changes if I was to truly begin living and release the pain and despair that was surrounding me every day. I could no longer keep the status quo. What I had been doing for years was not working any longer. I felt like the universe was giving me a sign to do something different. What that was I wasn't sure, but I knew I was in enough pain to begin exploring my options.

After leaving my job abruptly, with no game plan in sight, I took a couple of months off to focus on my emotional and physical health, both of which had suffered tremendously. I spent those first two months just sitting and meditating, journaling, reading and catching up on some much-needed sleep. I embraced and practiced the self-care that I had abandoned for years and began the process of healing from my life. This is how I began my journey to finding myself again.

It was a few months after my big life crisis that I created Soulful Connections. It came to me in my meditation practice and I began to realize I was missing a piece of myself that I needed to explore. Why couldn't I create a product out of those powerful questions that had helped me find my path? This deck of 120 thought-provoking questions was my way of helping people explore the deeper side of themselves and have more meaningful conversations. My intention was to get people to slow down, ask the big questions and listen carefully for the answers. It had saved my life, so it seemed only natural it could help others.

"Difficult roads often lead to beautiful destinations."
– Zig Ziglar

I created a signature workshop around these deep questions to help people access that part of themselves they had lost. I witnessed a beautiful example of this with someone in my workshop who was struggling to find their voice – their power. Sarah was complaining how her boss ruled with an iron fist and had unrealistic expectations. She didn't feel comfortable speaking up and was becoming resentful. During the workshop, she began asking herself, how am I contributing to this situation at work? Am I misreading what is actually happening? Am I making a story up in my mind about what is really happening?

Sarah was struggling with her life. Her young daughter was having health issues and her husband spent a lot of time travelling for work, so much of the household and family responsibilities were falling on her shoulders. Sarah was the oldest child in her family and spent much of her youth taking care of her siblings while her parents both worked. She carried this sense of responsibility into her adult life. Now was the time to look at what was working and what wasn't working in her life. We talked through how this was making her feel, what she needed to feel supported and how to verbalize to her husband her needs to have him be more present when he was home. She made a commitment to herself to ask for help at work. She realized she wasn't being vocal about being overworked and not understanding her role, which was constantly changing at the company. It was as if an invisible door opened and she found her voice and some clarity. Her fear and growing resentment had kept her stuck. She was avoiding the important conversation she needed to have. Her self-esteem was plummeting and she became disengaged at work and at home. It spiraled into her questioning whether she was even capable of doing her job, and whether she was happy at all.

We worked through different scenarios considering how to access her inner guidance so she could feel comfortable talking with her boss. I saw a sense of relief rush over her. She felt empowered and that week she spoke with her boss. He was relieved she had brought it to his attention; he valued her work and didn't want to lose her as an employee. They began working on a solution.

I wonder what would have happened with Sarah if she never explored her feelings? Would she have continued to blame her boss, her husband or herself? Would she have become complacent or left the company she once loved working for because she was afraid of asking for help? I've often said in my workshops that it's all an inside job. Every answer, every next move where you are searching for answers – it's all inside of you waiting to be accessed. If only we'd sit still, ask the questions and be patient enough to listen for the answers. We also have to do the work of becoming more fearless and have a willingness to do the sometimes painful work to create our best lives.

It's easier to run away. But that relief only lasts for a while. When we continue running and avoid looking inward to gain clarity on how we are feeling and what is causing us distress, we make knee-jerk decisions. If we can step back and take some time for self-reflection, we can find the answers that serve us well.

In this book, I share some powerful mind and body techniques and spiritual practices for accessing your inner wisdom and strength to help create balance, relieve stress, find your passion and purpose and turn your fear into faith. It is only then that we can begin to learn who we really are and what we are truly meant to be doing in this world. We learn how to lift ourselves and others up to become the best version of ourselves. We can communicate more effectively at work and at home. We learn how to work on a team with all different personality types and not be reactive. We can begin to respect each other's differences and celebrate new ideas, even if they don't mesh with ours. We start to let go of old stereotypes and embrace new ways of thinking and accomplishing tasks.

Life becomes more positive, and everyone around us benefits. It becomes contagious. Happy, well-adjusted people are a pleasure to work with and their infectious spirit rubs off on others on the team. There is a shift in culture and we all reap the rewards at home and at work.

Life becomes manageable, even a pleasure. And it all begins with finding the wisdom and strength that each one of us holds deep inside. Let it begin with me and with you.

Notes

1. What does it mean to be fearless?
2. What areas of your life are you afraid of or avoiding making changes in? Is there someone you need to have a conversation with that you are avoiding?
3. What is great about your life right now? What gives you the greatest sense of meaning and purpose? What can you do to create more of this in your life?

_____

_____

_____

_____

_____

_____

_____

_____

_____

_____

_____

_____

_____

_____

_____

_____

_____

_____

_____

_____

_____

_____

_____

_____

_____

_____

_____

_____

_____

_____

_____

_____

_____

_____

_____

_____

_____

_____

_____

_____

Chapter 2:
Stuck in the Mud

....

At the beginning of my self-discovery journey, I was in a lot of pain and was diligent in my newfound meditation practice. It was helping me feel better. I was learning the art of surrendering. I found my power to connect with a loving force of energy that went beyond my logical mind and my physical body. I was starting to get a true sense of who I was, and I felt deeply safe. I also reignited a solid journaling practice, exploring my hopes and dreams. I was spending a couple minutes every morning on my walk with the dog to list in my head all the things I was grateful for. It was a gratitude practice that made me feel happy for the little things and not focus so much on what I didn't have. But as I started feeling better, I began to slack on my meditation. I wasn't writing as much and I started spinning in my own mind.

After a few days of not meditating, I noticed I was feeling more depressed and worried again. The constant chatter in my brain returned, and it was hard to turn it off. That's when I realized what had happened. That day I made a commitment to myself to meditate every day, even if only for a few short minutes. I also picked up my other practices that had helped me through that difficult period of time in my life. I made a commitment not to get lazy or complacent again. There may be a day here and there where I slip but I won't let multiple days or weeks go by without reconnecting with my spiritual practices.

In the early days of my coaching practice, I noticed a reoccurring theme with the people in my workshops and retreats. Everyone was struggling with keeping weight off, fighting fatigue, mood swings and feeling burned out. I found I could tailor a weight-loss program to their individual needs and they would start feeling better for a short time and lose the weight.

My clients were happy to have more energy, and for some, they felt empowered to make even more changes to help themselves feel good. But for a lot of people, it was short-lived. How many diets, food restrictions and weight-loss programs have you been on in your lifetime? If you're over 40, it's probably been a few too many to remember. I can say the same. I've been there. My health problems and weight gain happened right before I turned 40. I was told by my doctor that it was probably hormones; it was my age; I needed to exercise more; try a low carb diet; etc. I tried it all. And it would work, for a while. But I seemed to slip back into feeling sick and tired. There was no diet in the world that I knew of that was going to make me feel happier, less stressed and more fulfilled inside.

I began researching and taking more courses on the body and mind connection. This became a big part of my coaching program. After my own life crisis, I came to realize, even more than before, that what we think, how we act, our stress levels, our happiness, and our family and work life have a large impact on our health, our weight and our overall well-being. If things are out of balance, we subconsciously self-sabotage our efforts at a healthy lifestyle. The stress, the resentment, the anger and the frustration all well up inside us and we look for ways to numb ourselves and find some happiness – even if it means doing or eating things we know we shouldn't.

When we live in a highly stressed environment, our cortisol levels remain high and our body becomes accustomed to living in the fight-or-flight scenario. If our bodies are in a constant state of survival mode, it's hard to feel or look good when you live in this state for a prolonged period of time.

This is when I made the shift for myself and in my coaching practice. I was no longer so much focused on the food we put in our mouths, but how we are living, thinking, working and playing. Don't get me wrong; kale and other superfoods are good for your body and will help increase energy. But it is just as important to our health to feed our mind, body and spirit.

In our society, we have an epidemic of feeling uninspired, fatigued, discontent, fear driven and burned out. And as we accept this as just a part of life, it will continue to get worse. It's my opinion that this isn't getting enough attention, and part of my mission is to change all that. It's time for us to get unstuck.

So how do we begin to make life-altering, positive, transformational changes? We can begin by looking at the background to unhappiness; it begins with the ego. Inherent in every one of us is the powerful ego. When I talk about ego, I don't mean that boisterous, self-inflated sense of self we often attribute to the ego. I'm talking about the ego that lies inside of us that diminishes us and keeps us in state of unhappiness. The ego creates separation, and that creates suffering. You know about anger, hatred and fear, but there are also subtler forms of negativity that are so common we often don't recognize them as such.

For example, impatience, nervousness, irritation and that feeling of "I can't take it anymore" is so commonplace for us that we don't even realize how unhappy we have become. Many of us spend a large part of our lives in this state, until we wake up and realize that underneath these powerful feelings, there are certain unconsciously held beliefs and thoughts that led to our discontent and latent resentment.

So how do you get to the bottom of your thought patterns? I've found in my workshops and retreats, it's helpful to explore common thought patterns that arise and cause suffering and pain. Some are unrealistic expectations about what we expect to happen or not happen.

Here are a few scenarios to explore; see which may apply to you:

"I need to achieve this or acquire this before I can feel successful and fulfilled. I am frustrated and resent that it hasn't happened yet. If I express my anger and frustration, maybe I can make it happen."

"I really wish you would do this (or stop doing that) so I can feel safe, peaceful, content and happy."

"I can't believe this is happening now. Why does this always happen to me? I can't be okay with this outcome.

I must change it somehow."

"I had something bad happen in the past, and if it didn't happen then I would be at peace now."

The road to happiness can be a bumpy one if we don't explore the above assumptions, thoughts and feelings. The ego often catches us off guard and we react. If we don't take time for self-reflection, we confuse these inner dialogues with "facts" and accept them as reality. Being at peace and being who you are, really are one and the same. The difficult part is realizing the ego doesn't want us to go along with this reality. Instead it says something like, "At some point, in the future, I can be happy and at peace, if this or that happens." It may say, "I can never be at peace because of things that have happened to me in the past. And I won't let that go."

"Sometimes I feel like I'm slogging through quicksand. Then I stop and remember I'm not stuck in the ground; I'm stuck in my thoughts."
    – Christine Porter

The truth is, no one can force us to think in a different way. We choose our thoughts whether consciously or unconsciously and this creates our internal self-talk. And our thoughts become our reality. What we focus on attracts more of the same. This is based on The Law of Attraction; the concept is that like energy attracts like energy. Let me explain. Your experiences always reflect your inner beliefs. If you are always being criticized at work, it's probably because you are critical and now have become the critical parent that criticized you as a child. It can be unnerving to see these patterns, but they often exist and it's important to look inside yourself and ask, "How am I contributing to this experience? What is it in me that believes I deserve to be treated this way and experience this?"

If you have grown up with a negative outlook on life and are looking for ways to prove to yourself and others that the world is a bad and difficult place, you will attract more of it into your life.

Being angry and feeling pessimistic will attract other people who have the same views as you do. It will be hard for you to find and surround yourself with upbeat, positive people because they won't want to experience your constant anger and frustration. Like attracts like. When we spend time focusing on the bad in our lives and not appreciating the good, we become defeated. Sometimes it's worth exploring a different path for yourself, or a different thought pattern.

As I experienced how this process worked, I began to live more intentionally and paid attention to my inner dialogue. I began living more of what I was teaching others. Our thoughts and our words create our reality. So, if I wanted to have a life filled with peace and contentment, I needed to start looking at what negative thoughts were spiraling in my head. I became the silent observer, and it was fascinating to witness. I forgave myself for not being perfect when I slipped up and rushed to judgement or had self-limiting beliefs. I catch myself now when I find myself saying "I can't do this" or "I'm not good enough." I also forgive myself when I make stories up in my mind about how a certain scenario might go.

I'm careful now about who I choose to spend time with because their thoughts and behaviors will have a direct effect on me. I don't watch a lot of news, and I caution people to do the same. It is designed to keep us in a state of fear. The more violent and negative the broadcast, the higher the ratings, but the lower our own frequency becomes.

I try hard not to spend too much time thinking of the future or dwelling on the past. Sure, I have goals; I'm hoping we all do. But they are only a road map to my current desires, not the end-all-be-all. The goals I had years ago are very different from the goals I have now. This is neither good nor bad; it is a part of the cycle of growth. Sometimes things happen differently than we planned for and it's good to be flexible and not let it derail us. I used to find a lot of security in planning for what might happen. That used up a lot of my energy and it was a false sense of security in thinking I could control everything that would happen to me or my loved ones.

To begin in the recovery from feeling stuck is to realize that you can be at peace right now, if you realize this is the only moment that really matters. The past doesn't define you unless you let it, and the future hasn't even occurred, so why focus on trying to control it? The sad truth is, people sabotage their own work, their own happiness, when they undermine or withhold help or information from others. In the corporate world, and in family life, this can have devastating effects on the people involved and the company as a whole. Sometimes we don't even realize we are doing it.

In our culture, we spend a lot of time labelling people and feelings as either good or bad. We have a lot of judgement around these things. It is a part of the human condition. We label people as beautiful, smart, outgoing, self-involved, obnoxious, greedy, full of themselves. A lot of this can stem from our own experiences of being labelled as children.

I remember as I was growing up, I was called a motor-mouth because I liked to share stories that I made up. As an only child, this was my way of interacting and finding companionship with the adults in my life. My family loved me and they thought it was a fun nickname. It was a way of labelling me. I found myself stifling a lot of my talk because I felt ashamed. It felt like I was annoying them. As an adult, it has served me well in my business because I love telling stories as a way to connect with the audience. But it took me a long time to get over that label and speak proudly.

I spent years being overly careful not to speak too much in meetings or at dinner parties. I didn't want to offend or take anything away from others at the table. I learned to let go of this label through my meditation practice as I was struggling to find my purpose and a new path. I would sit at the beginning of my practice and ask myself who am I and what makes me unique? I felt a sense of pride well up as the answer came to me. I am a speaker, a writer, a coach and a storyteller. Someone who enjoys sharing information and life experiences to help others.

That was empowering for me. I no longer think of that term motor-mouth as a negative. Now it means something far more powerful to me. I have the gift of storytelling, and that is part of my life's purpose.

I truly believe we can change our story at any moment. I did and you can too. We all have old tapes that play in our head, that keep us from moving forward in life and making some of the changes that are necessary to create the life of our dreams. Erasing those old tapes that keep playing in our minds and choosing to see things differently is within our grasp. While our patterns are well established, comforting and often seductive in their false sense of security, wishing them gone isn't enough.

I know this from my own struggles and have witnessed this in my coaching practice. The real key here is awareness. Can we be witness to the stories we continue to tell ourselves and begin to question their validity? Can we begin to catch ourselves during a strong emotion and take a pause to reflect on what is happening inside of us? If we can remember to experiment like this, we can begin to train our minds and hearts to become Soulful Warriors.

Choosing self-kindness, self-awareness, self-love and focusing on self-care is critical in creating your most extraordinary life. Many people think this is a selfish way to look at things. But in reality, it is the only way to look if you truly want to be healthy in mind and body and be able to be of service to those you love. So now is the time to get clear on your intentions, what makes you unique, finding your inner voice and finding your hidden power for your big life transformation.

Notes

Some questions to explore your own thought patterns.

1. What self-limiting habit would you like to give up?
2. What has life taught you about yourself?
3. What are you proud of?
4. What regrets do you have? Do you believe you can change them or forgive yourself?

_____

_____

_____

_____

_____

_____

_____

_____

_____

_____

_____

_____

_____

_____

_____

_____

_____

Chapter 3:
Where'd My Dream Go?

I had a dream, and then I grew up. How about you? Did life get in the way of your dreams? Or did you just give up? For me, I got complacent and even lazy at times. I wasn't very grounded, and I needed a false sense of security at all times in order for me not to be too frightened. I didn't spend a lot of time dreaming of a different life. Why should I? I had a financially stable career that afforded me a comfortable lifestyle and some creative expression. Trouble was, it just didn't seem to be enough. I felt like an imposter. I didn't feel comfortable in my career and slowly began to go through the motions and avoid my feelings.

As a graphic designer, I had to force myself to become a machine. No one had the patience to wait for the creative process; they needed their designs done as soon as possible. I learned early on how to crank out the work and make everyone happy. Except myself.

What I really wanted to do was write, teach, create and speak to groups. I wasn't able to even pursue this dream until I began looking at my fears and anxiety to see how unhappy I had become. I had to be fearless enough to change course, mid-life, and follow a new dream. But this took time and a whole lot of inside work. It didn't happen overnight, but the work was worth it.

"If you are facing in the right direction, all you need to do is keep on walking."
- Buddhist proverb

Self-doubt, fear and insecurity can be immobilizing for many of us. The lack of being consciously aware of where we are, what we are thinking and what we are doing is also a stumbling block to finding our passion and purpose. For some, finding their passion and purpose sounds selfish and self-indulgent. I would counter that not seeking it out is self-limiting and robbing the world of that special gift only you have. The world needs more dreamers, inventors and optimists living life fully and on purpose.

As Eckhart Tolle explains in his book *A New Earth; Awakening to Your Life's Purpose,* an awakened consciousness aligns us with our life purpose. We have both an inner and an outer purpose, according to Tolle. Our outer purpose changes with circumstances and involves time. Our deep inner purpose remains always the same: to be absolutely present in whatever we do and let our actions be guided by awareness and the awakened consciousness, rather than controlled by the egoic mind. We can fulfill our destiny and realize our purpose when we awaken to who we truly are.

What keeps us stuck and off track? Accumulation of years of pain stored in our bodies and subconscious is one factor. Fear of the unknown, worrying we won't be good enough or that we don't deserve our dreams. Venturing into uncharted territories and taking risks others see as foolish or dangerous can play a large role in our decision-making process.

Recently at a networking event, a gentleman asked me what I did for a living. When I explained my coaching philosophy, this book I was writing at the time and the product line I had developed, he started in with his opinions immediately. Before I could even get my last word out, he went into a speech about how things would not work out well for me. You see, he had tried some similar businesses in our city and it didn't work out for him. So surely, it wouldn't work out for me. I don't think he meant any harm nor did he seem jealous or angry. He did seem concerned that I was dreaming too big and this would lead to bad decisions, based on his past experience.

This gentleman is what I call a Dream Buster. You know that person. You probably have someone in your life that has done the same thing to you. The Dream Buster is the person, whether well-meaning or jealous, that will tell you all the reasons why your dream, your vision for your life, will not work out. If you're not careful, the Dream Buster will have you second-guessing yourself and maybe even giving up on your dream.

Don't let yourself or others limit your dreams. The only real limits on your dreams are the ones you set for yourself. You've heard the expression "I'm my own worst enemy." Many of us have an inner self critic that won't let us venture too far out from our self-imposed beliefs. We can be our harshest critic, and it's based in fear. When you pay attention to your self-talk, what does it sound like?

I bet you've had thoughts about not being good enough. You may have thought you were crazy to have that dream, and said to yourself; "Who do I think I am?" or "I could never accomplish that." Could you even imagine talking to a friend the way you talk with yourself? If you did, they probably wouldn't be your friend for long.

> *"Here's the truth. We exist on this earth for some undetermined period of time. During that time we do things. Some of these things are important. Some of them are unimportant. And those important things give our lives meaning and happiness. The unimportant ones basically just kill time."*
> — Mark Manson

Are you not living your dreams because you are too busy living your fears? Self-limiting beliefs keep us stuck in place. If you're not willing to try and possibly fail, then you are almost guaranteed to stay in an average life at best. Give yourself permission to live the life you want to live. You may not know right now what you want that new life to look like, but that's not an excuse. Now is the time to begin the journey of self-examination to find your purpose-driven life. You picked up this book for a reason.

Are you busy living someone else's plan? So many of us grew up being taught that you have to follow a certain course in order to be happy, accepted and fulfilled. It's almost like a societal rule book. The rule book goes something like this: we grow up and graduate high school, go to college or trade school, get married, get the dog or cat, buy the house, have the kids, work at a solid job and maybe even receive a pension. Take a vacation once a year with the family. Raise the kids, plan for the grandkids and go into retirement. Hopefully at this point, you don't have regrets and you've lived your best life. But what happens if you wake up one day and realize you don't want to be on that path anymore? What if it isn't your true path and you have unfulfilled dreams?

Too much of life is spent waiting for the right time, the right opportunity, the right circumstances, for the right people, for permission to be and have what we want in life, and for signs we are on the right path. We need to stop waiting to live. Life is too short to not spend time doing what you want to do to feel alive and fulfilled. At any time, with a little courage, patience and self-exploration, you can give yourself permission to start living your dreams today.

If you want to live a life of your dreams, it's important to focus on the present, keep your thoughts and feelings dialed in on what you want to experience, how you want to feel and what you want to accomplish. Become curious about what excites you. Try not to focus on what has happened in your past. Focusing on reasons why your dream can't happen, how you've tried and maybe failed in the past and getting caught up in negative self-talk will guarantee to hold you back from your dreams. Use what you have learned from the past; don't use it as a way to unconsciously keep yourself stuck.

Notes

Some questions to explore your own thought patterns.

1. What's your big dream for your life?
2. What's holding you back from this dream? Is it your thoughts or beliefs? Is it other people's thoughts and beliefs about your dream?
3. What's your greatest fear around this dream? Has it come true or is it a story you are making up in your mind to protect yourself?
4. What one thing or action can you take today to get you closer to your dream?

_____

_____

_____

_____

_____

_____

_____

_____

_____

_____

_____

_____

_____

Chapter 4:
Who's Driving This Bus?

....

Our beliefs are seen through the lens of our inner child. These are pretty much set at age five or six and continue to influence us throughout our adulthood. One of the questions we can ask ourselves is "What am I believing that is making me feel like this?"

I don't know too many people that grew up in perfect homes. Many of us grew up in troubled or somewhat dysfunctional homes where we learned to avoid conflict whenever possible. Do this long enough and you learn how to deny your feelings. If you can't trust others to meet your needs, why even ask? You become convinced you need to be strong enough to take care of yourself and handle any situation without help. The only problem with this is that we begin to lose touch with our feelings. Feelings are important. They are the most helpful link to our relationships with ourselves and others. They help to navigate the world around us. They are also the barometer for what is and isn't working in our lives. To deny or numb our feelings is to lose our sense of self.

I remember an exercise I used in one of my retreats. I asked the participants what it was they needed in their life that was missing. I then asked how it would feel to have it. Several people struggled as they tried to access their feelings. There were comments ranging from "I'm not sure what I want or need" to "I don't know how to express what I'm feeling except to cry or get angry."

This exercise I use is now so very important in all my work. It allows people the opportunity to see how they may be disconnecting from themselves to the point of not knowing who they are or what they want and need in life. I remember having those feelings as I began living my life on autopilot. It didn't even occur to me to take a hard look at my relationships, my job and what was making me so unhappy. I don't believe any of us should wait for or need a life crisis to stop us in our tracks to make us realize we may be heading in the wrong direction.

If you don't allow yourself to feel what is going on inside of you, you won't know where to begin with healing and growing. We continue going through life asking is this all there is? How can you pursue your hopes and dreams if you are spending much of your time feeling guilty, resentful, jealous, fearful or sad? We begin to develop habit patterns that perpetuate the same experiences that we say we don't want to have. We encounter more conflicts at work. We don't say "No, I'm sorry I can't do that right now" and instead, to avoid any perceived conflict, say yes, and later become resentful. Or we don't have meaningful conversations with our partners, and so we become annoyed and angry that our needs aren't being met. We have a short fuse with our children and they are left wondering why mom or dad is always so easily annoyed.

*"Your vision will become clear only when you
can look into your own heart. Who looks outside,
dreams; who looks inside, awakes.*

– Carl Jung

As human beings we have the potential to disentangle ourselves from old habits and thought patterns that are no longer serving us. I think in our hearts, we want to love ourselves and our neighbors. To work together to make the world a better place. To become more consciously awake and be free of negativity and judgement. To love rather than hate. We also have a strong inclination to stay the same, remain asleep and play it safe.

If we were honest with ourselves, do we see how our words and actions contribute to the suffering, pain and confusion of the world? Collectively we create a work culture that is either positive or negative. We foster a happy and fulfilled home life or one of quiet suffering. We surround ourselves with positive, life-affirming activities and friendships, or we wallow in negativity and self-destructiveness with like-minded people. The choice is always ours to make.

When we aren't in the trap of quiet desperation or fear, we intuitively know what the right thing is to do. If we aren't numbing ourselves or constantly moving with frenetic energy, and take pause, we can get in touch with that deeper side of ourselves that will let us know what will help rather than make us feel worse. Anger, fear, pity, cravings and jealousy will keep us from the deep intelligence that is within each of us. We can become masters of our emotional reactions, if left unchecked, can make us say and do some crazy things.

Before I woke up to myself and discovered a more conscious way of living, I was living a life of quiet desperation and panic. I had struggles at home that started bleeding over into my work life. I found myself behaving at work like I had never behaved before. My life was spiraling out of control, and I wasn't at the point where I had the energy or the tools to stop and look at how I was feeling and what needed to change. It was just easier to go with the flow and wait for some great miracle to appear and show me the way. And that did not happen. It wasn't until I found myself arguing with a coworker outside her office cubicle, demanding to know when she was going to start doing her job so I didn't have to, that I realized I had lost control. I'm not sure if I was asking to be fired, taking back a false sense of control or I just was feeling so overwhelmed and angry that I let it all fly.

After the heated discussion, I walked around the block to cool off and figure out my next move. I couldn't think straight I was so angry. Angry at my coworker, angry at my boss for overlooking all the dysfunction of the department, humiliated that I lost my cool in front of everyone and looked like a young child throwing a tantrum. At least I had the presence of mind not to start calling her names.

I always prided myself on being a professional at work. In that moment, when I walked away, feeling my blood pressure shoot through my head, struggling to catch my breath, I remembered the phrase "the first one who raises their voice loses the argument." What a horrible saying, as if we are always in battle to win. But the truth is, in that moment, I looked and sounded like someone I didn't even recognize and I wanted to win. I was caught up in being right and having control over the situation. It was not my proudest moment. I had spent months allowing my unhappiness to simmer. All I could think to do was complain about the long days and stress and look for ways to find a little joy when I left work. I needed that job, the stability, the paycheck, and God knows I needed the distraction from my personal life. Those were my excuses at the time for not taking care of business.

So, I took the easy way out, and an hour after my meltdown, I quit my job. It was a rash decision, with no safety net and no real direction as to what I was going to do. I struggled with the idea of finding another job, going back to my freelance business, moving out of state to start over. Start a whole new life in a new place. My marriage had ended, and I had a burning desire to escape. But I remembered the phrase "wherever you go, there you are." You really can't run from yourself. You can change your address, change your job, change your hair and your friends but you still have to deal with yourself. That's the harsh reality we don't like to think about.

This would require a lot of courage and faith in myself to find my way out of a really bad situation. Did I have what it takes? I was in so much emotional pain; my life felt so out of control and I was dealing with a lot of anxiety and depression. I had to dig deep and find the courage to figure out my next step. There was no looking back. I couldn't stand the thought of continuing one more day living like I was living. Numb and checked out. Later I would realize I had given up and abandoned myself.

While I don't regret leaving my job, I do regret the way it happened. And the hurt and embarrassment I caused my coworker. She definitely didn't deserve my anger and my hostile confrontation. I wish I had the openness to stop, breathe and take a break to slow the process down. We all have that time to take pause, take a break and reflect on why we want to say that mean thing, become aggressive, make a nasty call, stick our heads in a box of candy or take a drink. It's true, in those heated states, we believe doing those things will bring some relief. That we will have some sense of satisfaction and comfort and feel better in the end. When we pause and ask ourselves "Will this action make me feel better when it's over?" our wise inner self will tell us what we already know: we won't feel better in the end. We will only make matters worse.

If our initial reaction in the heat of the moment is to fly off the handle or react immediately, it means we have been cultivating a habit for years. And we've gotten good at it. Whether it's a form of deflection, or fear of being exposed and not looking "perfect," or we just can't handle our strong emotions, this is when it becomes important to go within and look at what your story is. Let your life become an experiment. Pause and become witness to how you are feeling, interrupt the usual chain reaction and don't spin out of control. The goal is to not strengthen the fear and aggression habit we've become accustomed to.

We don't need to make the other person or ourselves the bad guy. When you sit and pay attention to what you are feeling, explore where it is coming from, look at your past and how you might have been triggered, it becomes easier to make changes. You don't have to be held hostage by old internal programming. It's enough to just be an observer and make a commitment to do better next time. Pausing creates a barrier between being totally self-absorbed by our feelings and creating space to be awake and fully present.

To face ourselves, with all our pain and circumstances, we can begin to look compassionately at our minds. When we are courageous enough to become familiar with our habits, we no longer feed those habits that don't serve us. We aren't being swept away in the pain of highly charged emotions. We become more open and accepting of ourselves and others. That's the gift we can give to ourselves and the world.

Notes

Some questions to explore your own thought patterns.

1. What areas of your life feel out of balance?
2. Is there one area in your life that you can begin to work on to create more harmony and balance for yourself?
3. How would it feel to make the positive changes needed?
4. What's holding you back?

_____

_____

_____

_____

_____

_____

_____

_____

_____

_____

_____

_____

_____

_____

_____

_____

_____
_____
_____
_____
_____
_____
_____
_____
_____
_____
_____
_____
_____
_____
_____
_____
_____
_____
_____
_____
_____
_____

Chapter 5:
Finding Your Inner GPS

....

I know I'm not the only one who's had some hard times in life and struggled to find their way out. In some strange way, there may be comfort for all of us to know we are all in this together. Everyone has struggles, no matter how wonderful their life seems from the outside. We all struggle with fears, anxiety, regrets and bad decisions. It's part of being human. We also share a deep longing to feel connected, useful and fulfilled. To have a passion and a purpose in order to feel as if we have truly lived.

When was the last time you leapt out of bed feeling energized and ready to embrace your day? Once you feel like this, even if only for a few hours or days, you crave that feeling, and it makes every other day look rainy and gray. To feel this way is to feel truly alive. It's the vast difference between eating a fast food meal in front of the TV watching endless reruns or dining on a delicious four-course meal at a five-star restaurant with your favorite person.

When was the first or last time you asked yourself: Am I truly living and following my life's purpose? Do I know what that is and how to access my wise inner self to explore it? Am I willing to go to any lengths to find my purpose and present my true self to the world? Am I willing to explore my hidden fears and anxiety and begin to release them? How badly do I want to feel really good and live my dream life? How long am I willing to wait to begin living my dream?

Is it time to begin the journey home? That's the essence of this book and the work I do. Helping folks find their hidden compass. When I ask people in my retreats why they are here, most of them say they want to find their true selves, their passion and purpose. To come home to that hidden piece of them that they haven't been able to access in years. To feel whole, less afraid and to feel a sense of peace and balance. To feel a sense of true joy and excitement in being alive.

We actually can cut off our source of aliveness when we deny what is in our hearts – our passion and purpose for living. This happens when we give up on our dreams to take a safer path, when we disconnect from ourselves and get caught up in the rat race of making more money, desperately seeking a feeling of safety and security at any cost, doing what is expected of us rather than what we are called to do. We become the walking dead. We can go through the daily motions of working hard and providing for our families, but that isn't truly living; that's existing. It doesn't mean it will be easy, and you won't have difficulties or some suffering, maybe even meet with some defeat, but you won't have as many regrets trying to make your dream come true. I'm not saying we should all quit our jobs tomorrow and go chase that dream. But every day, there are steps we can carve out to get us closer to doing what we love to do. First, we have to invest the time in ourselves to find our right path.

As humans, we struggle sometimes with following our heart and our direct experience and instead, we listen to the advice and instruction of others. How is it we come to believe that others know what is best for us, rather than using our own internal guide? I remember in college loving my journalism classes and thinking I would love to be a creative writer and focus on special interest stories for magazines. I allowed that dream to get shot down in my last year of college when I was told all the reasons it probably wouldn't be a good idea for me. I was told it was a competitive field, I may not have enough talent to make any money at it and I should look for more lucrative career options. I took this advice and to this day I have regrets. It has taken me three decades to find the courage to start writing again.

Knowing your purpose is when you feel at home, when you feel the most alive and connected with what you're doing. When was the last time you had this feeling?

Why do we disregard simplicity, patience and compassion for ourselves and others?

In an age where we tend to run from our feelings, and don't lead with our hearts, we can make the mistake of reframing what living with simplicity, patience and compassion means. Don't let your mind confuse simplicity for stupidity, patience for laziness or compassion for sentimentality. These are worthwhile traits to explore in an effort to live a whole-hearted, fulfilled and happy life.

Simplicity refers to direct living, first-hand experience, where we touch and feel life directly. It restores us. Patience also gets us closer to our source and living whole-heartedly, with intention and purpose. We live in such a fast-paced society where there is a sense of everything being an emergency, when in reality, very little is. I bet you can see this firsthand in your day-to-day affairs. It's no longer enough to receive emails at all hours of the day; now we text coworkers at all hours. I can't even tell you how many emails I received in any given day that were flagged as emergencies. The phrase "We need it ASAP" was so commonplace to the point of no longer having any great importance. How could it? It's overused and abused and has become undervalued. Every day we are trained to put out fires. And not just in the office but at home. Our kids are overstimulated and overscheduled just as much as we are.

You can begin to ask yourself if these are real emergencies, someone else's sense of emergency or self-imposed emergencies. Become witness to your habits and the habits of others and shift directions when you can. How many times have you gone on vacation and brought your computer to check email? How long did it take for you to wind down before vacation could actually begin? For me, it was usually the last two or three days before I could let go of work mode. I can't even tell you the battles I had with my partner about unplugging and leaving work behind while on vacation.

This isn't good for our relationships or our work. Burnout is a very real condition many of us suffer. Even when you are loving your job and everything you're doing each day, it's important to disconnect and have down time. It really does make you more efficient and productive when you return to your work. It also trains people to respect your off time. Meditation, mindfulness and self-care are some of the ways you can begin to make yourself a priority and not exist on the bottom of your to-do list.

I've come to realize the importance of simplicity, patience and compassion. Without them, life can crush you.

You can't find your heart and soul in your intellect. It resides in a deep, heartfelt place inside you. Following your intuition and feeling your heart's purpose can be scary at times. You may have to give up your persona, your title, your financial security and other people's expectations as you move in the direction of your dreams. This can cause a lot of fear as you place your trust in the unknown. I remember sitting in my living room a few days after I quit my job, fear racing through my body as I thought, what have I done? I've just committed career suicide – or worse, financial suicide. I live in a small city where a lot of talented people I knew were financially struggling in their own businesses or trying to find good jobs. Surrendering to the unknown and not trying to control every next step was a large and necessary lesson for me.

Even with that fear racing through me, I knew I would somehow be okay if I just trusted that I was being guided to something even better. At the time, I wasn't sure what that bigger plan was, but I knew that if I didn't follow the path, if I didn't explore what would fulfill me and make me happy, I would be filled with regrets. I didn't want to live a life of quiet suffering and sadness. I was tired of feeling so depleted, frustrated, angry and living the same lie day after day. I wanted to feel alive and be excited about what I was accomplishing with my life. I wanted creative expression and to give back to others who might also be struggling. I made a commitment to myself to not let my fears paralyze me. No matter how hard I tried, I couldn't avoid the fear of letting go of control. Sitting with the fear was the first step on my journey.

So many of us struggle with being unclear on what we want, confused as to what to do next with our lives. We drift along, complacent and numb, unhappy with our life circumstances but not sure how to make empowering changes. We feel stressed and overburdened, overwhelmed to the point of not caring anymore – or becoming angry and resentful. I remember that feeling of being so stuck that I would think in circular patterns, ruminating over and over again the same scenario, hoping for a different answer. It became maddening, not to mention exhausting.

Life doesn't have to be a continuous grind. There doesn't have to even be any earth-shattering, career changing or family upheaval, to begin the journey to feeling better and understanding who you fully are. It may be as simple as changing your perspective, going inward and seeing what your triggers are and how to overcome them. It could be that you need to find a way to ask for help because you are overburdened. Or find a way to express yourself so you can be heard at home. It could also be as simple as sitting quietly with yourself for a period of time to find balance and calm so you can make better life decisions instead of waiting for things to implode around you.

On the following pages, I will dive into some techniques and spiritual practices that I began exploring to help me find my inner guidance. I was desperate to find out what I was meant to be doing. I knew deep inside I was missing a key piece of myself and I wouldn't be okay until I found it. I believed that there had to be a reason my whole world was blowing up, and it wasn't just bad luck or bad karma. There was a deeper reason, and I needed to find a new path if I was to create an extraordinary life. Life doesn't have to be and certainly shouldn't be the struggle I had been making it. I struggled with letting go, always focusing on others and their problems, and getting swept up in the drama of the day. These were great escapes to keep me from doing the work to figure out what I needed, what I wanted and what was best for me.

A spiritual path springs forth from a daily routine that reaffirms our personal connection with a purpose or a way of life. Practicing compassion, gratitude, appreciation, forgiveness, generosity, meditation and taking care of your wellbeing can all be a part of your spiritual life. If you are new to exploring your personal spirituality, remember that this is a process. I'm not necessarily referring to anything religious, although it's your choice if that works for you. Taking time to cultivate a spiritual practice tends to include habits that promote healthy living. Follow what leads your soul and you won't be led astray.

I encourage you to try these techniques I've outlined in the next chapters for several days and see how you can begin to access a part of yourself that might have gone missing in action, to reconnect with yourself on a deeper level. That is where your power center lies. Try carving out a few minutes each day to get acquainted with your amazing self. It all begins with the wisdom of you.

I hope you can find your balance, gain clarity on your true purpose, release the stress you've been carrying, and cultivate compassion and acceptance for yourself and others. Then you can begin to live your true authentic self.

Chapter 6:
The Power of Meditation
The Original Inner GPS System

....

"The most important relationship you will ever
have is the one you have with yourself."
— Mel Robbins

Sitting quietly has never been easy for me. As a Type-A person who is always on the move and hyper-focused on getting everything done immediately, the thought of sitting quietly on a cushion in the lotus position, trying to erase thoughts from my mind for an hour or more sounded painfully excruciating. This was not something I wanted to entertain for myself. Still, I knew meditation could be good for me. I had read plenty of scientific, medical and spiritual articles on the emotional and physical health benefits of meditation. The research was intriguing. The studies outlined the changes I could expect: lower blood pressure, stress reduction, improved cognitive thinking, more focus, better sleep patterns, a greater sense of calm and a more positive outlook on life.

I tried listening to podcasts on how to meditate while driving to work, hoping I could reap some benefits just from listening. "Tomorrow" was always the promise I'd make to myself to begin a practice. Tomorrow would come and go but it never seemed like the right time. I made a lot of excuses that felt reasonable—I'm busy, I'm too stressed, I need to plan my morning meetings, I'm trying to get a little more sleep, too many family responsibilities, and on and on. Why was I so stuck? Why couldn't I just try? There was no major cost in participating and it seemed everyone who had a meditation practice seemed more calm, relaxed and happy. To think you can accomplish all of this just from sitting quietly and erasing all thoughts. But wait; how could you erase thoughts? Who is able to do that? How do you do that?! I tried sitting on the floor cross-legged like the yogis. That became uncomfortable and I became obsessed with the proper body alignment of my spine. Was I breathing correctly? Deep, cleansing breaths felt forced. How do I sit here and look and feel at peace? Silly, but that's how much of a perfectionist I am. I tried in bed in the early morning hours before work and promptly fell back asleep. One day I decided to move to a chair but my racing thoughts and to-do list got in the way. Feeling like a meditation failure, I decided this wasn't going to work for me.

It wasn't until a day when I was in emotional distress and sick of being depressed that I started rethinking this meditation thing. I was in the doctor's office for the second time in two months complaining about weight gain, not sleeping well, stress at home and work. I began tearing up as I described the feelings of being overwhelmed, sad and frustrated at my job. I remember thinking I needed to make some changes or I would end up really sick. Meditation seemed like a good place to start. Maybe, just maybe.

Meditation seemed elusive and mysterious to me, but at its core, it really is about getting in touch with a deeper part of ourselves. There is a small inner voice inside all of us that knows exactly what we need and when we need it. Some call it intuition, our "source" or God working through us. Whatever we call it, it truly is the original GPS we can trust to guide us in the right direction—if we allow it space to be heard in our busy lives. Getting to this core at first might seem challenging but with a little commitment and the desire, anyone can do it.

Meditation is the original "mobile device" that can be done anywhere at any time. Even in the grocery checkout line. Why is meditation so important? It helps us let go of familiar thoughts, old behaviors, stagnant emotions, and sometimes even relationships that no longer serve us. For most of us, leaving the "familiar" and stepping into the unknown can be a terrifying place that we try to avoid. This is why change is so hard and we often try and keep the illusion of control in our lives to avoid feeling scared. It's also the number one reason it's so important to make your meditation practice a part of your daily routine.

So where do we begin? There is no right or wrong way to meditate. The most important thing to do is get still. That's it. Simply get still. Finding the way to quieting your mind comes with time. The notion of erasing all thoughts and clearing your mind is not really achievable for many of us—unless of course you are a Tibetan monk living in a monastery. And who wants to erase all thoughts and feelings anyway? The goal is to have a different relationship with your thoughts.

Don't judge them as good or bad, but simply become the observer. As thoughts enter your mind while meditating, you will begin to see what is pressing on your mind and what might need attention in your life. Even the most painful ones hold important information for us. It helps to acknowledge, reflect and recognize the feelings and thoughts so we can make better, more informed decisions on what is best for ourselves. They are the road maps for our lives. Ignoring or denying them usually leads to suffering in the long term.

There are so many expectations for us first-time meditators and it rarely goes the way we had planned or hoped for. Try not to be discouraged or frustrated but find the beauty and excitement in the thoughts, feelings, memories and fantasies that are jumping around your mind, wanting attention. These are the clues to connecting with your true self. What is your true self? Maybe it's the part of you that you left behind years ago as you chased your career; or put all of your energy and time into raising a family; or just took a different, unexpected life turn. All are a part of who you are and they hold great importance; no judgement here. Do you know what motivates you now? What you crave and need to feel more settled in life? What makes you smile and feel like you created something special for yourself and others? What's your purpose? What makes you unique? Where do you want to be a year from now, five years from now? What's the next step? Do you know? That's what meditation offers: insight into your life, your purpose, your hopes and dreams.

What if you just sat in a quiet space for a few minutes and began to take notice of your thoughts as they enter your mind? What if you became the silent observer and noticed what arises with each deep breath you inhale? "Acknowledge, review, accept and bless it" has been my motto. No judging. Release the urge to be the perfect meditator, to do it right. Calming the "monkey mind," that incessant chatter we all hear, and starting to focus on our breath and asking life's big questions. Who am I? Why am I here? What is it I'm being called to do with my life? Asking these questions of myself helped me get a clearer picture of my life and how I viewed the world. It doesn't always happen overnight and it can feel really uncomfortable to be alone with ourselves. Turn off your computer and smartphone. Just sit quietly. Don't worry about the outcome or trying to do it perfectly. Let go of the attachment of how it will get done; just set the intention to try.

I wanted so badly to be the person who meditates. I knew it somehow would make a difference in my life. How I had been living wasn't working. It wasn't getting me any closer to finding out who I truly was, outside of my profession and my family's opinion, and what I really wanted or yearned for in my life. One morning I woke up and decided to give myself a 30-day meditation challenge. I wasn't exactly sure how I would begin my meditation practice or how I would sit still for even five minutes every day, but I was determined to try. Every day I woke up a little earlier than usual and went and sat in my cozy chair and closed my eyes. I tried silent, deep breathing meditation one day. Another day I tried a guided meditation I found on YouTube.

Once I faced my fear, sat quietly on a regular basis and began listening to my intuition, that little voice inside me that was begging to be heard, I found the right path I needed to follow at that point in my life. It helped me discover my dream, and I launched Soulful Connections. Many of the questions that helped me find my true calling, I included in the Soulful Connections card deck. I began realizing that what feeds my soul is helping others find their way out of pain, anxiety and unhappiness and find their power and purpose so they can begin to create lives they love. I think it takes courage to break from the norm, ask the big questions and really show up for our lives.

This is the only life we have, in this body and at this time. We all deserve to be heard and seen. It only can happen when we are ready to show up for our lives. How to do this? Stop and sit in the stillness. Ask the big questions. Listen for the answers. The Wisdom of You is begging to be heard. Go and follow those big dreams that lie inside of you. I will be by your side cheering you on!

30-Day Awareness Meditation Challenge:

There are many forms of meditation; walking meditation, seated quiet meditation, chanting, the list goes on. One of the most gentle and approachable forms for a beginner is mindfulness meditation. The object is to observe the wandering thoughts as they drift through your mind. The intention is not to get too involved with the thoughts or judge them but simply be aware of them and then let them pass.

1. Set a timer for 5 minutes.

2. Sit comfortably in a chair, on the floor or a cushion. Try not to lie down; chances are you will fall asleep.

3. Close your eyes gently. Soften your mouth and make sure not to clench your teeth.

4. Make no effort to control your breath, just breathe naturally and fully, expanding your stomach with each inhale. Exhale fully through your nose.

5. Focus your attention on your breath, observe how your body feels. Breathe into the tight areas and sink deeper, letting go of any areas that feel restricted.

6. If your mind wanders, observe the thoughts and release them as if they are on a cloud drifting by or in a rushing stream. Return your focus back to your breath.

Repeat this meditation each morning before you start your day or in the evening before bed for a full 30 days. Increase your meditation time as you become more comfortable with your practice. Try inserting a few minutes throughout your day to achieve even greater results. For a quick break at work, close your eyes as you sit at your desk and breathe deeply for a few moments, focusing only on your breath. In the car on your commute to work, pay attention to your thoughts and try and slow them down by breathing deeply and saying a calming phrase such as: I relax into my day with ease.

Chapter 7:
Self-Care is Love

"Isn't it time to begin your journey from surviving to thriving?"

— Christine Porter

Self-care is a huge part of what's missing in the life of a busy, stressed-out overachiever, and everyone in between. That was me a few years ago. I was so busy climbing the corporate ladder until one day I just decided to leave. I was excited to start a new chapter and create my own business. Then it became the need to work crazy hours to get my own business to become a success. The busyness continued as I began setting even bigger goals for myself. I struggled with my home life and friends, trying to keep everyone happy and healthy. I tried to always be there to cook and clean and be the counselor, doctor and advisor. It became routine for me to forget about me, except for the occasional massage or dinner out with friends. I taught myself not to put my needs first. I didn't pay attention to how I was feeling, what I was eating or who I was spending time with. All of these things created burnout. I became overweight, chronically fatigued, annoyed, stressed, moody and sleep deprived. There never seemed to be enough time or money to do or have the things I wanted. Sound familiar?

We've all experienced these symptoms from time to time. We're all human and life gets in the way. But when it becomes a way of life, a sustained way of living, it becomes a chronic problem we can't afford to ignore. Our nervous system becomes overtaxed and we live in a hyper state of arousal, shooting cortisol, the stress hormone, through our bodies on a regular basis. This leads to chronic fatigue and eventually chronic illnesses.

What exactly is self-care and why does it sound so selfish? Self-care is the practice of deliberately taking an active role in protecting your own well-being and happiness. In its purest form, it is the willingness to pay attention to your thoughts, feelings and needs that ensures that you are being cared for by you. Not in a selfish, narcissistic way but a way that allows you to be true to yourself. Self-care is about knowing your worth and developing and maintaining a healthy relationship with yourself which helps to produce positive feelings and boost your confidence and self-esteem. It helps you stay sharp, motivated and healthy in body and mind. You can't give to anyone else what you don't have inside of you. One of the healthiest gifts you can give yourself is the permission to make taking care of your daily well-being a priority.

I used to think self-care was selfish, something only people with a lot of money and time on their hands could even think about. It seemed self-indulgent and out of my reach. That was my thinking many years ago. Since then, I've changed my tune a bit. I began to realize that for me, self-care wasn't about weekly trips to the spa for massages and manicures (although those are nice from time to time). It was something more accessible, easier, less expensive and often times more fulfilling. It was a requirement I set for myself to begin living a healthier life.

I have been practicing self-care right at home on a daily basis now and most of the people in my life will tell you I'm a much better person for it. For me, taking a few minutes out of each busy morning to meditate, journal my thoughts and drink my favorite cup of tea is a form of self-care. Those 10 to 20 minutes I spend sitting in silence and checking in with myself are priceless. Journaling about the past day, week or month, are important in helping me sort out my thoughts and feelings. It gives me something concrete to reflect back on. If I get stuck, I pull a question card from my Soulful Connections deck and see where the question leads me. The minutes I spend alone with myself can be an eye-opening journey.

Every morning I take my dog for a walk around the neighborhood. I used to think I did it for him, but I love the time we spend in nature, listening to the birds, letting the warm sunshine fall on our faces and saying hello to my neighbors as they come out on their stoops to pick up their morning paper. Is this a form of self-care? You bet. It's meditation in motion, and I cherish the time I get to have a deeper conversation with myself in nature. Not to mention the quality time I get to spend with my favorite pooch, Bodhi.

My yoga practice is self-care. The healthy food I choose to eat is a form of self-care. Going to bed early, choosing to take myself to a movie instead of spending more time on the computer working, talking gently with myself and others—these are all forms of self-care. Self-care boils down to any activity that we do deliberately and with intention to take care of our mental, emotional and physical health. It is not a selfish act. It is an act of self-love and self-worth that improves our mood and helps to reduce our anxiety as we begin to honor and care for ourselves.

Give yourself permission to let go of all the unrealistic goals and busy work that keep you in a perpetual cycle of feeling overtaxed. Making time to nurture and care for ourselves can sometimes be difficult. We all have busy lives, but self-care is the catalyst to creating a life you love filled with purpose and meaning. We all have an inner wisdom, a guidance that knows what is best for us, and we need only to tap into it. Each one of us has different needs that when met, make us feel cared for. The challenge for each of us is to find the balance in our lives and the supportive activities that help us move from surviving to thriving.

In my workshops, I like to spend some time with folks talking about what their ideas are for self-care. It's usually an eye-opening moment for many people as they struggle to think of ways they actually take time for themselves. I ask people to write down some activities they've been wanting to do but haven't made the time for. For many folks, it's as simple as wanting to read a book they bought months ago, getting to the gym, trying a new restaurant with an old friend or watching a movie with their partner. We humans are good at making excuses as to why we can't make time. Burnout and numbing out are on the rise. With today's technology, we feel like we are available to everyone at any time, and it's becoming more of an epidemic to forget about ourselves. How about you? What areas of your life might be begging for some balance?

30-Day Self-Care Challenge:

Here is a list of a few exercises in self-care that you can begin working on today. Choose one or two each day if possible. Explore your thoughts and feelings around each one of your self-care exercises and journal your experience. It may be uncomfortable at first, but it will become easier with time. When you take time for yourself, you will reap the benefits of feeling more centered, loving and patient, and much less frazzled and depleted.

1. Knowing who you are and setting limits is at the core of self-care. Self-care means noticing when you are doing more than you are used to handling and looking at ways to slow things down and setting priorities. What one area of your life can you say no to and make space for a few minutes of down time?

2. Knowing how to rest and not overdoing it. Do you know how much sleep your body needs in order to feel refreshed and rested? Are you sleeping at least that much? Self-care means making a serious effort to make that happen and allowing yourself the rest you need.

3. Making sure you're well fed with the right foods. Do you eat foods that are good for you and give you the energy you need to function at your highest level? Do you take a few minutes at every meal to truly enjoy your favorite healthy foods? Or are you snacking on high-carb, high-sugar foods in a mad rush during the work day? Self-care means being mindful of what you put in your mouth and how it makes you feel. It also means setting up every day eating routines that provide some "down time" to enjoy healthy foods.

4. Resting your mind. What is it you do during and after your work day to rest your mind and decompress? What helps you tune out the noise? Try stretching for a couple minutes at your desk or take short brief walks throughout the day. Drink plenty of water, chat with a co-worker or friend for a couple minutes or listen to some soft music. This will help you refresh your mind and body.

5. Setting boundaries at work and at home. Is there anything at work that can be done to make your work less stressful? Are you always volunteering for the special projects? Are you refusing to ask for help or extend deadlines when necessary? At home, are you the one everyone in the family turns to for help or expects to cook and clean? Practicing self-care means being able to ask for help when needed, saying no when necessary, knowing where your boundaries are and speaking your truth.

6. Knowing who you are. Self-care is being able to recognize your own temperament and what is possible for you to achieve. Know what you like and don't like and what is acceptable. If you are a highly sensitive, empathic person, recognize when you are experiencing sensory overload. Identifying your triggers and planning accordingly can help lesson inevitable stress.

7. Taking time to have some fun! Begin making a habit to do something that you can look forward to every day, or at least each week. It doesn't have to be complicated. Maybe it's reading a good book, getting a massage, making a meal you love or going to a movie with a friend. Self-care is learning to enjoy the little things in life and making a serious effort to make them a habit.

8. Feeding your spiritual self. Whether you pray, meditate, commune with nature, practice gratitude or wake to see a beautiful sunrise, find that something that is inspirational to you and embrace it.

9. Taking time to love yourself. Acknowledging there is only one you—that you are unique and perfect just the way you are. Write little notes to yourself expressing your joy at who you are, what you've accomplished and what makes you special.

10. Asking for what you need. Who do you need to have a meaningful conversation with and ask for help today?

_____

_____

_____

_____

_____

_____

_____

_____

_____

_____

_____

_____

_____

_____

_____

Chapter 8:
Journaling for Clarity

....

Today is the day to set your dreams in motion.

From a young age, I found my creativity in writing. My short stories were a way to entertain myself–not always an easy feat when you're an only child. But writing was a way for me to explore my world and create new ones that suited my personality and my moods. As a kid, I wasn't always great at expressing myself and asking for what I needed or wanted. Most of the time, I wasn't even sure what I needed or wanted. Writing gave me that outlet to explore who I was and how I viewed my world. When I was a teenager, a diary became one of my best friends and allowed me to confess my innermost secrets. Knowing I was the only one reading my diary gave me permission to express my thoughts without the fear of being judged. Now that was real freedom of expression.

What's the one thing you can do right now to gain clarity, explore self-expression, tune into your feelings and turn your dreams into reality? Journaling. Or call it your diary if it feels right. No matter what you call it, it's about exploring who you really are. And there's more. Studies have shown that a regular journaling practice helps to clear your mind and focus on your goals. Getting your thoughts, feelings and aspirations down on paper offers you the opportunity to build a deeper connection with yourself and identify goals and desires you want to manifest in your life. Plus, it's inspiring to go back and reread past entries and see how far you've come in your life journey.

But really, why journal? Journaling promotes self-knowledge, decreases stress and can facilitate emotional healing as you improve self-awareness. It also provides a creative outlet that many of us may not have otherwise.

> *"Journal therapy is all about using personal material as a way of documenting an experience, and learning more about yourself in the process," says Kathleen Adams, LPC, a Colorado-based psychotherapist and author of Journal to the Self. "It lets us say what's on our minds and helps us get—and stay—healthy through listening to our inner desires and needs."*

Some people have challenges when first starting a journaling practice. I've heard people say they don't journal because they don't feel like they are good writers or they struggle to find the words to fill a blank page. We tend to judge our writing as either good or bad. We think we need perfect sentence structure, impeccable grammar—or even just the story to make sense, as if someone might read it. It becomes exhausting and feels like another thing on our to-do list. Sometimes we can get stuck not even knowing where to start with a journaling practice. Or maybe you've started so many times but haven't been consistent.

What if we let go of the need for perfectionism? What if we didn't worry about if our entries rambled? Or our feelings and thoughts seem scattered or we judged them as unfounded, callous, insensitive or just plain silly and childish? Isn't that in itself enough to begin our self-exploration?

Journaling isn't about writing poetic passages or the next great novel. It is more about expressing your feelings, even if it means jotting down the random thoughts we have that moment. Setting aside a few minutes a day to journal provides a way to keep track of what you want to remember, and it helps you deal with tough situations and dig up new ideas. Some days you may be inspired to write pages; other days it may just be a few words. The benefits are there either way as long as you stop and pay attention to how things are going. Let's take the pressure off journaling as a practice and maybe look at it as a way to get in touch with your creative side and begin some self-exploration.

30-Day Journaling Challenge:

1. Try writing first thing in the morning when your mind is most quiet. Just a few minutes and a few thoughts each morning and you're on your way to a journaling practice.

2. Don't worry about writing in complete sentences. Try a stream of consciousness where you write about everything and nothing in particular. Start by writing phrases or simple words to describe your mood or feelings.

3. Use journaling prompts. A journal prompt is a question or topic that gets your mind flowing. If you're struggling to find things to write about, try picking a card from my Soulful Connections deck and journal your answer. There are 120 "big life" questions that are meant to help you explore life on a deeper level. This is a great way to start your journaling each day.

4. Journal every day. Even if it's just a few sentences, the more you write the easier it becomes.

5. Cultivate an attitude of gratitude. Every time you journal, list all the things you are grateful for in that moment. This helps reframe your mind and the way in which you approach life. Positivity, even for the smallest things you have, attracts more of the good stuff you crave.

_____
_____
_____
_____
_____
_____
_____
_____
_____
_____
_____
_____
_____
_____
_____
_____
_____
_____
_____
_____
_____
_____
_____
_____
_____
_____
_____
_____

Chapter 9:
Healthy Eating Rules

....

Take care of your body;
it's the only place you have to live.

Ever since I was a kid, I've had a love affair with sugar and carbs. Bread and cookies were my go-to foods. This addiction carried over into my adult life where I began developing health problems as a result of too much indulgence. I remember feeling really run down and achy. Unfortunately, feeling lousy is the new normal today, and people are just accepting it as a way of life. But I was really sick and tired of feeling sick and tired. I didn't understand what I call the "food/mood" connection that was causing my low energy and mood swings. I was also having trouble losing weight around my midsection. I knew I needed to make big changes in my diet. I began changing my eating habits, and that helped quite a bit. I learned in my holistic nutrition school that it wasn't always enough to just eat "healthy" foods. For some of us it's an undiagnosed food allergy. A sensitivity to gluten, soy or corn. The "battle of the bulge" can be hormonal or stress related. Or it could be an overconsumption of sugar.

In my workshops, I share a few statistics that often lead to gasps from many in the group who had no idea how their so-called healthy foods were hijacking their health and weight. Did you know the average American consumes 185 pounds of sugar a year? That's six to eight cups consumed in one week! Sugar is hidden in so many packaged and processed foods that we don't even realize we are eating so much of it. We may know candy bars, donuts, soft drinks and specialty coffees contain a lot of sugar. But what about the high levels of sugar hiding in places you'd least expect it? Salad dressings, condiments, crackers, soups, cured meats and diet meals are frequent offenders. Some of the worst culprits are protein bars, many of which are really candy bars in disguise. Most processed food—everything you buy in a package—contains sugar, in one form or another. Low-fat foods and fat-free snacks often have more sugar than the original food, because manufacturers use sugar-based products to replace the original fat content.

That's one of the reasons I created the Healthy, Sexy & Fit™ program during my one-on-one health coaching days. My clients saw real changes. They lost weight, had more energy and let go of the brain fog. The best part was after about two weeks, they reset their palate and their cravings disappeared. It takes a little time but the benefits are worth it.

What we put into our mouths directly impacts our mood. Did you know that in America today, once you reach adulthood, up to 80 percent of your health is based on lifestyle and food choices?

You've probably heard the term "Frankenfood." It may have piqued your interest, or maybe you even laughed at the phrase. Unfortunately, it is a term that describes much of the processed food we are eating on a regular basis. Food isn't what it used to be. I remember drinking Coke as a kid in the seventies and it had real cane sugar. Now, Coke is made with high-fructose corn syrup, an ingredient far more toxic and unhealthy than pure cane sugar. But it is a less expensive sweetener for the soft drink manufacturer and even more addictive. Today, there are millions of dollars being spent by food manufacturers to develop new, more addictive products.

Early on in my coaching practice, I developed my Food Rules to help my clients improve their digestion, clear up skin issues, increase energy and lose some weight. The following is a list of my Food Rules that can help you make better choices and take the guess work out of healthy eating. No diets or strange foods are required, just a willingness to become curious, explore new ideas and inquire about where your food comes from.

Food Rule #1:
Eat regularly. Don't skip meals. When you go too long without eating, your blood sugar drops, setting you up to make poor meal or snack decisions when cravings hit, leading to binging on sweets and carbs.

Food Rule #2:
Don't eat anything that has a shelf life longer than your lifespan or is delivered through your car window. The amount of chemicals, additives and poor-quality ingredients are a staple of junk food and fast food. They are highly addictive with their high levels of sodium, sugars and gluten and offer little nutritional value. They are designed to make you overeat, and you won't feel

satisfied for long.

Food Rule #3:
Try to avoid any foods with ingredients you can't pronounce or recognize. If you don't recognize the ingredients, they were made in a lab and most likely not something you should be consuming for a healthy lifestyle.

Food Rule #4:
Don't eat food that was made in a facility where everyone wears masks. This includes fast food restaurants and packaged meals from the store. Many are filled with chemicals and preservatives manufactured to increase the flavor to promote over-eating. Instead, choose whole, unprocessed foods. They will also fill you up, leaving you feeling nourished rather than craving more, which is what happens when you snack on wasted, empty calories.

Food Rule #5:
Eat lean proteins and good fats with each meal. This helps control blood sugar. Organic free-range eggs, smoothies with berries, nuts, veggies and protein powders are good examples of mixing protein and healthy fats.

Food Rule #6:
Visit the produce aisle of the supermarket and shop abundantly for foods that grow in nature and eventually rot. Avoid the interior aisles where the processed foods, sauces, dressings and snack foods are located. These are mostly the simple carbohydrate foods loaded with sugars, low quality oils, fats and chemicals.

Food Rule #7:
Cook more at home. The more you prepare your own food the better. You can control what goes in and there won't be

any hidden sugars, additives or gluten to spark cravings.

Food Rule #8:

Get your fiber from fresh fruits, vegetables and seeds and not from sugary, overprocessed fiber and protein bars.

It's the only body you have, so show it some love and feed it well!

Always check with your doctor to make sure there aren't any underlying illnesses involved in making you feel sick and tired.

30-Day Healthy Eating Challenge:

1. Begin reading the labels on everything you buy. Can you understand and identify the ingredients? If not, leave it alone.

2. Start your day off with a superfood smoothie. Include berries and greens to get lots of antioxidants. For lunch, make a healthy salad that includes lean protein and veggies with your own homemade dressing. Looking for recipes? Log on to my website at PeaceandPear.com, visit the store section and download my clients' favorite recipes from my Healthy, Sexy & Fit™ program for free.

3. Try one new fruit or vegetable this week and discover new ones to add to your daily menu.

4. Try a delivery meal kit service. There are so many new ones that cater to different tastes and eating styles from organic vegetarian to paleo. It saves time on grocery shopping and menu planning, and many offer nutritious, all-natural foods you prepare yourself. Not all are created equal, so do your research.

5. Skip the candy and protein bars for an energy boost and opt instead for a Kind Bar. Or make your own trail mix with raw nuts, seeds and a few raisins or dark chocolate for sweetness.

6. Keep a log of what you eat each day and review at the end of the week. I bet you will notice you are eating out and snacking throughout the day more than you realize. Try to curb this by eating high-quality foods and bringing your own snacks.

_____
_____
_____
_____
_____
_____
_____
_____
_____
_____
_____
_____
_____
_____
_____
_____
_____
_____
_____
_____
_____
_____
_____
_____
_____
_____

Chapter 10:
Finding Your Balance

....

You will never find time for anything.
If you want time, you must make it.

My years spent in the advertising industry left me feeling burned out and overly tired. Like many people living on this planet, I kept pushing myself with unrealistic deadlines and demands without thinking twice about how it was impacting my emotional and physical health. It was the office norm to work 60 to 70 hours a week, and it was expected. Later, when I began my freelance design business, I found early success and had more client work than I knew what to do with. Before I knew it, I was recreating the agency life, but now I was doing it on my own. I was spending long hours working on several projects and weekends off were few and far between. When I went on vacation with my husband, I always had my laptop and had to check emails regularly. I was nervous I'd miss something or a client would have an emergency or rush job, and I didn't know how to say no.

This obsessive work pattern bled over into my personal life and my husband became distant and resentful. I was stressed out trying to please everyone, never really looking at whether I was happy and enjoying life. I wasn't paying attention to what was happening with my family. It's so easy to fall into this trap, until one day there is a life crisis or a health issue that wakes you up to your frenetic life. My life crisis was poor health and a deep exhaustion that I couldn't treat because I always had more work to do.

As a coach, I learned early on that what works for one person doesn't always work for another. But the one common denominator for all of us is that if one area of our life is out of control it most likely is impacting other areas of our lives. I believe it's important for everyone to find their own path to feeling balanced and whole. I don't believe anyone can find the magic formula for another person. What I can do is provide an awareness through asking some powerful questions that can lead to real solutions. In my workshops we explore life balance, where we feel connected with ourselves and with our environment in a synchronized way.

When I talk about balance, I'm not only talking about your work and home-life balance. I'm talking about all areas of your life working in harmony together as much as possible. There are several components that make up our lives as a whole, and sometimes we forget the importance of balancing these areas. It's important to look at your work, family life, finances, hobbies, education, spirituality, friendships and beliefs. When these components that make up our life are out of balance, we become overwhelmed, stressed and numb.

How do we know when our lives are out of balance? Here are some questions you can ask yourself:

Do you have little or no time for your important relationships, such as family and friends?

Do you often work overtime and engage in regular work-away-from-work?

Do you take few or no breaks while working?

Do you have any interests or hobbies that you engage in on a regular basis?

Are you experiencing difficulties in sleeping or getting enough sleep?

Are you aware that you are eating the wrong food and/or eating out too much?

Do you consume too many stimulants, such as coffee and sugar, throughout the day and need alcohol at the end of the day to wind down?

We all have periods of time when we are overindulging and finding we could check all the above on the list. But when we are living this on a regular basis, life becomes out of balance, and it might be time to take a good look at what needs changing and rearranging.

Have you ever sat down and examined the various areas of your life only to realize that some areas get most of your focus and other areas are neglected? What are your life priorities and how do you reach your goals? If you neglected some areas, is that impacting your fulfillment and life satisfaction? Is it sabotaging your goals?

It's okay if finding balance means spending more time in one area, as long as the other areas are still appropriately supported and functioning at the same time. In other words, balance may not mean that each area gets the same amount of focus, but none of them should ever get left out, or worse, forgotten.

The subtle art of slowing down allows you to not only savor your experiences, but also it allows you to fully focus your attention and energy on the task at hand. It may seem counterintuitive, but moving at a slower pace lets you get more things done more efficiently, while rushing diminishes the quality of your work and your relationships. Slowing down lets you be more mindful, deliberate and fully present. When we slow down, we are giving ourselves the opportunity to reacquaint ourselves with the natural rhythms of our bodies and our lives.

30-Day Finding Balance Challenge:

1. Avoid checking your email upon waking, giving yourself time to settle into your morning. Instead, try doing some gentle stretches with deep breaths or going for a brisk walk outside.

2. Make a list of all the things you've been putting off until a later date. Examine your list and choose the most important ones. Create a strategy to do it yourself or ask for help.

3. Make a game plan for having fun. Starting today, what one small thing can you do to put a smile on your face? Is it listening to your favorite comedian at break time? What about going to see a movie with a friend or your partner? How about planning that vacation you've dreamed of? Can you make time to go out for your favorite meal? Maybe it's as simple as calling an old friend and catching up. Whatever it is, make a commitment to yourself to recharge your batteries with some fun.

4. Make a list of all the important areas of your life and rate them from 1-10 (10 being the best). Look at your list and examine what areas in your life need attention and find ways to make an impact.

Chapter 11:
The Art of Mindfulness

....

*Cultivating a practice of calm
amidst the chaos of life.*

Have you ever arrived at your destination only to realize you don't remember the drive? Or what about having that pit in your stomach when you realize you just polished off a whole pizza in a matter of minutes and you weren't even hungry. Maybe it's being distracted with your to-do list spinning through your mind and not being able to focus on a conversation with your partner. We've all been there, and it can be startling when you catch yourself. These are classic examples of being distracted and unaware of what is going on around you in the present moment. Our minds take flight, we lose touch with our body and soon we're engrossed in obsessive thoughts about something that just happened, worrying about what happened in the past or what might take place in the future.

*"The present moment is filled with joy and happiness.
If you are attentive, you will see it."*
                                              – Thich Nhat Hanh

How time flies by when we aren't paying attention. Today more than ever, with the help of technology and smartphones, we are becoming more disconnected from ourselves and each other. According to the first-quarter 2018 Nielsen Total Audience Report, nearly half of an adult's day is dedicated to consuming content. In fact, American adults spend over 11 hours per day listening to, watching, reading or generally interacting with media. That leaves us little time for real in-person connections.

We are expected and have trained ourselves to be available and ready to respond at a moment's notice to work, our families and maybe even our friends and associates. This hypervigilance can cause us to feel scattered and overwhelmed while trying to juggle too many things at once. And usually not doing any of those things well. It's becoming an epidemic, and we have to work hard to find the space to breathe and unwind. Sometimes this takes days on vacation or a retreat to finally unwind and get our lives in balance—until we go back home again to our lives and start the process all over again.

What does your typical day look like? Have you ever really thought about how you are living? The distractions are probably endless. Do you plan your day while listening to music, drinking coffee and commuting to work? In the rush of your day, are you losing your connection to the present moment and not aware of what you're doing and how you're feeling?

Practicing mindfulness is a simple practice once it becomes familiar and routine for you to check in with yourself throughout your day. There are smartphone apps to program alerts to "check in" with yourself. Mindfulness is simply the ability to be fully present, in that moment, fully aware of what you are doing, where you are, what you're thinking and feeling and not being overly worried or reactive to what's going on around you. Practicing this concept of living in the moment makes it easier to savor life's little and big pleasures, and that creates a greater sense of well-being. We become less preoccupied, more productive and find it easier and more satisfying to form deep connections with others.

"The subtle act of being present in the now begins with a mindful, subtle shift in slowing down our thoughts and our actions."
— Christine Porter

"Living in the present moment" is another term for mindfulness. However you frame it, mindfulness can offer a sense of freedom, a lessening of stress and responsibility of carrying too much. Another way to look at it is becoming an observer of your life where you become an actor rather than reactor. An actor is someone who takes initiative. A person who sets a course for themselves rather than becoming reactive and having their emotional stability rocked at every turn or whim of others or their circumstances.

Life happens while we're trying to control it. We can become more at ease and release fear and sadness when we stop trying to label everything as either good or bad; or scary or sad. What if we see it as a temporary pause, a universal lesson to learn from, or a personal self-reflection moment? We can take pause, practice a little mindfulness and remind ourselves that everything is just as it should be in this moment. Explore the smells, tastes of the present moment, breathe into that sacred stillness and give ourselves the space to just be.

Mindfulness techniques start with the basics of our everyday life. You don't need to find a separate time or add another activity to your to-do list. You can practice mindfulness techniques at any time in any environment, even if it's loud or crowded. It can also become your go-to, on-the-spot stress management strategy. Practicing mindfulness will help reduce your anxiety almost immediately.

> *"What mindfulness is saying to all of us is,*
> *Find your own way. Listen to your own heart.*
> *Listen to your own longing."*
> – Jon Kabat-Zinn

Finding peace, joy, connection and compassion for yourself and others doesn't have to be just a lofty goal. You don't have to be Buddha. Simply take a pause and do whatever you are already doing in this very moment with full awareness, mindfully.

30-Day Mindfulness Challenge:

Pick two or three of these exercises to try each day. Mix and match or add on as you go. Soon they will become a part of your daily routine you enjoy.

1. Do a mindful body scan. Upon waking in the morning, take a few deep breaths. Wiggle your hands and toes and get in touch with how your body is feeling in this moment. What areas are tight and stiff and need stretching? What areas feel loose and supple? What about your mindset? What feelings are you experiencing?

2. Practice positive affirmations. A great mindfulness habit, affirmations are positive phrases that you repeat to yourself or write down on paper and review throughout the day, describing who and how you want to be, using the present tense, as though the outcome has already occurred. Here's an example of a positive affirmation: "Everything is working out for my greatest good. Life supports me and I am safe, I am loved and I am powerful." Establishing a positive affirmation habit first thing in the morning and again in the evening before bed can impact the outcome of your entire day. When practiced deliberately and repeatedly, positive affirmations change the chemical pathways in the brain in a positive way.

3. Practice mindful driving. When you get into your car, take a few deep breaths. Don't turn on the radio or create other distractions while in the car. Turn your phone on silent. As you begin to drive, make an extra effort to notice your surroundings. If you get stuck in traffic or someone cuts you off, notice the feelings that arise (anger, frustration, anxiety, competitiveness), and simply identify them. Use traffic stops or other necessary stops to practice a few deep,

calming breaths. Once you arrive at your destination, after you've turned off the engine, sit for a moment and take three deep breaths, really letting go on the exhalation. Do you find yourself feeling more relaxed and aware of yourself?

4. Focus on your work purpose. Why do you work at your particular job besides the obvious, to pay the bills? Can you approach your work with love and purpose, no matter how challenging, uninspiring or difficult it may be? To be mindful of the purpose of your work allows you to be more fully engaged with the tasks you perform. Finding the positive in your work allows you to explore a more positive outlook about your job and your life.

5. Cultivate a beginner's mind. Develop a willingness to release preconceived notions about the way things should be based on your existing knowledge or beliefs. With a beginner's mindset, you temporarily suspend all of your opinions, knowledge and strongly held beliefs so that you can explore an idea without mental limitations. Your mind becomes open to possibilities and that opens the door to new thoughts, feelings and experiences for you to explore.

6. Take a walk. Working at a desk all day and sitting too much is unhealthy. Schedule periodic breaks throughout the day to get up from your desk and take a five-minute walking break to clear your mind. If you can, go outside in nature for your walk. Nature can be grounding and place us back in harmony. Notice the sights and sounds and how your body feels in the fresh air. What sounds are you hearing? How blue is the sky? What does the sun feel like on your skin? Recognize that each snowflake has a different shape and size. Follow the flakes with your eyes, watching them as them land.

7. Practice a "shut-down" ritual. Your actions in the 30 minutes to an hour before bedtime can make or break your ability to fall asleep quickly and impact the quality of your sleep. That's why I like to suggest a mindfulness habit of creating a soothing, sleep-inducing ritual before pulling up the covers and turning out the light. Sit or lie down in the stillness and breathe deeply, slowing your brain down. Explore listening to a guided sleep meditation or some soft music that will allow you to slow down your brain and release the mental chatter.

_____

_____

_____

_____

_____

_____

_____

_____

_____

_____

_____

_____

_____

_____

_____

_____

_____

_____

_____

_____

_____

_____

_____

Chapter 12:
Finding Your Purpose
Exploring your curiosity

....

*"Let yourself be silently drawn by the strange pull
of what you really love. It will not lead you astray."*
— Rumi

What's your dream? That thing that burns deep in your soul and begs to be heard. It starts with a whisper and sometimes you can hear it whenever the noise in your head quiets long enough. We all have dreams, hopes and aspirations. Our soul is crying out to be heard. Over time the screams get louder and the flames more intense. This is the point where we either follow our hearts and chase that life dream or we squash it, becoming numb, disengaged and keep the status quo. When we begin to lose our soul-purpose, we may feel stuck and unhappy.

I've seen the latter happen all too often with my friends and myself. For years, I squashed my passions and dreams because I was too afraid of what might NOT happen. I was stuck in the fear of the unknown and it felt really uncomfortable. I had a hard time sitting still and letting my mind take a mental break from the anxious thoughts. I was so used to fixing, doing, forcing, strategizing, making plans, changing plans, that my thoughts and my life were frenetic. I couldn't think straight half the time. Sometimes we become so disconnected from ourselves that we don't know how to listen to that inner voice, let alone begin to act on it.

> *"Your mind is constantly looking for excuses.*
> *Stop listening to them and get on with your life."*
> – Christine Porter

I spent most of my life listening to what others thought of my career decisions. I wanted the house, the dog, the yard, the nice car, the pretty clothes, the vacations and the ability to not have to worry much about money. I wasn't living a rich lifestyle but I was comfortable. Unfortunately, "comfortable" meant being numbed out and not really paying attention to whether I was happy and feeling fulfilled in my job and my life.

My life had become so out of balance that I began developing bad habits just to escape the pressure and pain. I remember I kept a steady diet of coffee, sugar, packaged foods, sandwiches and donuts left over from the early morning office meetings to give me the energy to get through my day. There were a lot of wine-and-cheese happy hours with colleagues as we decompressed from our long, pressure-cooker days. The only exercise I was getting was the walk from the parking garage to the conference room for daily morning meetings. My relationship began to suffer because we stopped talking about anything real or meaningful. At the time, I felt like it took too much energy, and it was easier just to dump the day's details about long meetings and unrealistic deadlines as we ate our dinner mindlessly. The television blared in the background for some form of entertainment and distraction. I would fall into bed and wait for the next day to come to start the grind all over again. The only thing worth repeating each morning was hitting my snooze button.

Those were really long days. I know I'm not the only one that felt that way. There was a lot of stress. There was great anxiety and a general feeling of dread that hovered over my days. Ever felt like that? It's uncomfortable, and if you live with that feeling long enough, you begin to pick up bad habits. I started emotional eating and drinking to help ease the stress and frustration. We say we are "living for the weekends," but when the weekend comes, we are preoccupied with all the errands and chores we neglected during the week. We struggle to work in some small pleasures. Maybe a movie, a dinner out or a long nap— a reward to ourselves for making it through another long week.

"It is the denial of death that is partially responsible for people living empty, purposeless lives; for when you live as if you'll live forever, it becomes too easy to postpone the things you know that you must do."
— Elisabeth Kubler-Ross

I believe we all have a purpose. A unique gift that only we can offer the world. Whether it's becoming a novelist, a nurse, a mentor to teens or a floral shop owner, all of these skills and talents are needed in the world. Identifying, acknowledging and acting upon this is critical in becoming your true authentic self. We may find it in our current work, or maybe we start a journey of self-exploration into another part of ourselves that we may feel is missing.

Sometimes finding this passion and purpose isn't always easy. Some people are born knowing what they want and how they will achieve it. Some of us take a different path and may need a little help figuring it all out.

Finding your passion, your purpose is the biggest gift you can give to yourself. We are all born with a deep, meaningful purpose that resides inside of us. Isn't it time to discover yours?

So where to begin? We can begin with asking life's big questions and exploring our thoughts and feelings around them. This begins the catalyst for change. When I created Soulful Connections, my intention was to heal myself. I was asking myself some thought-provoking questions, trying to take the time to really reflect on the answers and what they meant for me. I soon became aware that I had been denying a large portion of who I was. I was playing a role I had fallen into years before. It wasn't until I quieted my mind and stopped focusing so much on my obsessive thoughts that I was able to gain some clarity on what steps I needed to take in my life. It's hard to feel happy, content and fulfilled when you aren't living your life's purpose.

Living your life's purpose is about doing what you love to do, doing what you are good at and accomplishing what is important to you and what you feel passionate about. When you are living your true purpose, the right things, the right people align with that vision and help you achieve your purpose. How do you know when you are living your purpose? The more joy, peace, excitement and contentment you feel, the more you know you are following your dream and your purpose. We all have an inner GPS system that will give us signals if we are on or off our right path. Getting in touch with this inner guidance is key in finding what makes you unique and how you want to express yourself. These all point to your power and purpose in your amazing and unique life.

30 Days To Finding Your Purpose Challenge:

1. Explore the things you love to do and what comes easy for you. What puts a smile on your face? Write these things down in your journal and refer back often.

2. Create your own mission statement or a life purpose statement. Take some time to think about what your world would look like if it were operating the way you envisioned it. Be clear, brief and keep it exciting and positive. Ask yourself:

   • What are the top 3 qualities I value?
   • What is my calling; my life's aim?
   • What inspires me the most?

3. Sit quietly and meditate on the question "Who am I and what am I meant to be doing with my life?" Journal your thoughts and feelings that arise during this meditation time.

4. Create a vision board filled with pictures, images and phrases that make you feel good and put a smile on your face. Keep this board in a space where you will see it often. This helps you focus on the positives and what you hope to manifest in your life.

5. Set aside 20 to 30 minutes to make a list of all the times you've experienced true joy in your life. Begin to look at the patterns in your list. You should be able to find a common theme that can draw you to your passion and purpose.

6. Ask your close friends and family when they've seen you the happiest and filled with passion and purpose.

_____

_____

_____

_____

_____

_____

_____

_____

_____

_____

_____

_____

_____

_____

_____

_____

_____

_____

_____

_____

_____

_____

Chapter 13:
Vulnerability is Your Strength

Being vulnerable to life opens you up to your true potential. It is where you find your power and purpose.

> *"When something moves you emotionally, trust and know you're on the right path. This emotion, whether anger, sadness, happiness or fear, holds important information for you to explore. Don't ignore it.*
> *Lean into it and embrace all the spaces you may fear."*
> – Christine Porter

From a young age, I remember feeling scared and afraid. This caused me to never participate in sports or theater or anything where I might be ridiculed. I remember being called a perfectionist but deep down inside I was scared to show up and be fully seen. I always worried I wouldn't be good enough or be laughed at so it became easier to fall into the woodwork. It wasn't until later, after a couple years of therapy, a few dozen self-help books and enrolling in a coaching program that I learned my perfectionism and procrastination stemmed from my internal fears. A fear of not being good enough, not being smart enough, not lovable enough and certainly not worthy of lofty goals like my friends had.

My parents divorced when I was very young, but even as a small child I remember feeling unsafe and scared much of the time. Maybe it was the tension in the house, the arguing and not enough loving talk; or maybe it was all the moving we did, and all the new schools where I was the new kid over and over again. Maybe it was my family not having a lot of expectations for me. Or maybe it was the ADHD that plagued me in middle school. Or the hearing problem that almost kept me back a grade. It could be all of those things—or maybe none. And does it matter as an adult what the cause is? Many of us suffer from fears that force us to play small and we may not even know why. I can tell you one thing, one of the most frequently asked questions in my workshops is: "What if it doesn't work out for me and I fail?"

We all have fears. Just like animals, humans are hardwired for it. It serves a purpose in our lives and protects us when we get close to danger. Fear can also keep us stuck. It can keep us from following our dreams or taking a chance that could provide for a better life. We stay stuck in our fears and try so desperately to pretend to have it all together to avoid feeling vulnerable. This robs us of truly living.

Today, we are overstimulated, over-caffeinated, over-dramatized and surely over-anxious. We are surrounded by messages of fear when we watch the news, violent television shows or reality TV shows that exploit the worst part of humanity. Almost every day there are new reports on rising global temperatures, an increase in cancer rates, a scarcity of resources and global markets tanking. It's in the collective consciousness to perpetuate the idea that there is not enough, and we should be fearful of our future. We fight hard not to feel vulnerable as we try and suppress our fears.

In *Daring Greatly*, Brené Brown describes vulnerability as "uncertainty, risk and emotional exposure." It's that unstable feeling we get when we step out of our comfort zone or do something that forces us to loosen control. Our fear sets in.

Being willing to let yourself be vulnerable takes great courage, and we can often fear we are losing our sense of self. The moment a situation makes us feel vulnerable, our first impulse is to do everything possible to escape it. It's an inherent aspect of our survival instinct. It takes courage to be vulnerable in new situations and new relationships.

What if instead of trying to avoid our vulnerabilities and fears, we actually embrace them? With a little introspection, our fears can help us grow. They help us get to know ourselves on a deeper level if we let them in. We begin to learn more about who we are, what makes us tick and what is important to us. They also show us areas where we may need to focus some extra attention and love in order to heal. Practicing mindfulness is one area I needed to work on.

Letting go of control and not trying to plan every aspect of my life became liberating. I was moving out of fear and trusting that the right solution, the right idea, money, safety, friendship—it will all be there. This shift requires having faith in yourself that all will be well and will work out exactly as it should for your greater good, even if you can't understand it right in that moment. That doesn't mean we never feel scared or have self-doubts. It's important to let yourself feel the feelings but staying in that place, not making any changes, is not healthy. Thoughts, feeling and actions all help manifest your destiny. What you focus on grows.

Why do we get stuck looking into the future? Part of me gambles that by worrying in advance, bad news will be easier to face if it comes. But worrying will not protect me from the future. I am not a fortune teller, and I don't know what will happen in the future, so why spend today worrying? It will just keep me from living here and now. So when I find myself leaving the present and panicking about the future, I've learned to remind myself that the future is not today's problem. Don't make up stories in your head; it will only make you more anxious.

Fear is a closed door. Never let fear make your decisions. Few good decisions come from a place of fear, unless of course you are contemplating jumping out of a plane without a parachute. Fear keeps us stuck in the same old routine. Fear keeps us in the mind patterns that got us here in the first place. If you let fear take over your mind, you won't be able to truly live. You will stay stuck in place. Fear keeps us wondering what might be, and it keeps the good stuff in the future, never to materialize. Fear creates stress in the body and mind. And we know today the body and mind connection is strong.

Don't let your subconscious run the show. Sometimes you just have to tackle your fears, no matter how uncomfortable, if you want to change your life story.

30 Days To Overcoming Fears Challenge:

1. Ask yourself, what would you do if you weren't afraid? Make a list and look at your answers. Are your fears valid or is it a made-up story in your head?

2. Imagine your biggest fear and imagine if you were starring in the movie with your fear playing out. Imagine the worst-case scenario and figure out what you would do in this situation. You will feel better prepared for the worst case, which most likely will never happen.

3. Write it down and then prove you're wrong. Get your journal and write down what you are afraid of. Can you begin to recognize how your mind is bullying you into believing those fears? A few days later, go back and review. Much of the time, our fears seem melodramatic. Write a rebuttal to your fear. Summon your inner defense attorney to defend you. See how you feel lighter and more powerful.

4. Sometimes the best and only thing we can do is dive into our fears. Break your fears down into small, bite-sized chunks. Practice overcoming a little fear and work your way up to the bigger ones. This will give you more courage to keep going.

Chapter 14:
The Power of Gratitude
Opening the Door to a Happier You

....

"Gratitude makes sense of your past, brings peace for today, and creates a vision for tomorrow."
— Melody Beattie

What does it mean to be truly grateful? Gratitude is the ability to let the little things that would normally bore you suddenly thrill and excite you. It's looking at each moment as a small gift and see it for the magic that it truly is. It's saying a big thank you to the universe.

What are you grateful for in this moment? If you're having a tough time answering that question right now, it's even more important to ask it. The reality is, there is always something to be grateful for. I used to struggle with this concept when I was in a lot of emotional pain with my divorce. I became hyper-focused on all the things that went wrong and the ugly way we reacted to each other. It became a habitual thought pattern during that year. It wasn't until I began looking at my thoughts and how they were impacting my mood and how I related to the world, that I put the pieces together. I needed to think more positively by appreciating what I did have, so I could begin to feel better about myself and my world. I was also able to start looking at what I wanted and needed to make my life my own masterpiece rather than just going along for the ride.

I took this gratitude concept I was beginning to live and created a powerful workshop around it. I began to see real change in the folks who participated in this workshop experiment. I received emails from participants explaining how they took the principles and started their own daily gratitude practice. They said it helped them shift from feeling out of control, wanting more to make them feel good, to being thankful and present in their lives.

When we take the time to ask ourselves what we are grateful for, certain neural circuits are activated. Production of dopamine and serotonin increases, and these neurotransmitters then travel neural pathways to the "bliss" center of the brain. This process is similar to the function of many antidepressants. Practicing gratitude creates feelings of contentment as we sit in the present moment.

In positive psychology research, gratitude is strongly and consistently associated with greater happiness. Gratitude helps people feel more positive emotions and appreciate good experiences, which in turn improves their mindset and their health. It also helps us cope with adversity better and build stronger relationships.

When our boss says "thank you" to us, we feel more valued and appreciated. This makes us feel good. When we express to our partner how much we like the little things they do or acknowledge how special they are to us, we create greater happiness and appreciation in our relationships. Small gestures done routinely often have more of an impact on us than a less frequent grand gesture.

Gratitude improves psychological health. A regular gratitude practice also reduces a multitude of toxic emotions, ranging from envy and resentment to frustration and regret, according to Robert A. Emmons, Ph.D., a leading gratitude researcher and founding editor-in-chief of *The Journal of Positive Psychology*. His research focuses on the psychology of gratitude, joy and grace. Emmons has conducted multiple studies on the link between gratitude and well-being. His research confirms that gratitude effectively increases happiness and reduces depression.

Gratitude keeps you in the present moment, where you can truly be present and enjoy life. The more you practice gratitude, the more automatic it becomes. And in scientific terms, the more times a certain neural pathway is activated and neurons fire together, the less effort it takes to stimulate the pathway the next time, and those neurons wire together.

A gratitude practice can help you create a new life. Practicing gratitude doesn't always come easily, but changing your thought patterns helps to shape your outer world. We don't want to become victims to our life. Consider asking yourself the questions "What would it be like to…?" or "I've always wanted to…"

When you begin asking these questions you engage the frontal lobe of the brain, the brain's workshop, where we speculate, invent and create. You begin to set your intention, develop ideas around this thought. Feelings are created, and you find inspiration. You begin to emotionally condition your brain to this thought, and it creates a positive memory. By creating a positive memory, you begin to feel gratitude. Now you have to put action to it. You have to stay conscious and take steps toward this thought. Review the actions that haven't worked well in the past and create new ones. Developing new behaviors creates new results. Keep your energy up; limit toxic habits, people and chronic self-defeating thought patterns with a daily practice of gratitude. Acknowledge the good and bad of the day, recognizing that the obstacles may be guiding you in an even better direction. Now that is something to be grateful for!

30-Day Gratitude Challenge:

1. Begin a gratitude journal, or simply include a gratitude section in your current journaling practice. At the end of each day before going to bed, make a list of at least three things you are grateful for. Think of the lunch you had, your easy commute, a few extra minutes snuggling with your dog or meeting a great colleague at work. The list can be endless. As you continue this practice, it will become even easier and you will find that you are thinking more positively and sharing your appreciation with the world.

2. Set aside 10 to 15 minutes (or longer if you can) for a gratitude walk. Pay attention to the sights and sounds around you and see how many things you can be grateful for. Make sure to breathe and pause and say a little thank you for everything you see and hear. This is a powerful tool for shifting your mood and opening yourself up to the abundance of the universe.

3. Appreciate your partner or a close friend. Consider writing a thank-you note or finding other ways to show you care. Each of us has an innate need to feel valued and appreciated. Imagine what it is like to be in that person's shoes and explore their reality. This shows compassion and consideration that will make both of you feel good.

4. Take a moment out of your busy workday to thank a colleague or your boss. It builds camaraderie and creates a more pleasant workplace when we show compassion, respect and thoughtfulness for each other.

_____

_____

_____

_____

_____

_____

_____

_____

_____

_____

_____

_____

_____

_____

_____

_____

_____

_____

_____

_____

_____

_____

_____

_____

Chapter 15:
Believe in Something
Bigger than Yourself

Whatever it is, trust that you are being guided and supported. I first heard this phrase during a 12-step meeting. I was new to the group and seeking some support and guidance to figure out how to deal with a family member's addiction. I came to talk about their problems, how it was impacting me and what I could do to make them stop the self-destructive behavior that was tearing the family apart. In the weeks and months that followed I sat in those different rooms each week, and what I came to learn was that I couldn't make my loved one stop doing anything they were determined to do. I wasn't responsible for them or their actions. The only one I was responsible for was myself. I knew this on a conscious level, but subconsciously I was trying to manipulate situations to work out the way I felt they needed to. This was a highly ineffective strategy. It was exhausting, stressful and painful for everyone involved.

That's when I decided to take back my power and focus my attention on myself and what I needed to make my world okay. Not in a narcissistic way, but in a way that

I could begin to believe that I wasn't giving my peace of mind and my power away to someone else.

Much like the workplace or in our families, we can become subject to having our day hijacked by other people's agendas, their moods and their whims if we aren't paying attention. It's very easy to get caught up in other people's drama and to try and control the situation. We become reactive when triggered and can forget that there just may be a greater force working outside ourselves.

This is where I began to explore my world. What do I believe in? Is everything just a coincidence or are things happening for a reason? When I decided to slow down and reflect on how even the most difficult life events led me to a place of self-discovery and growth, I began to believe that random events may not be that random.

I've come to believe that everything happens for a reason. When I look back on some of my biggest moments in my life, the good and the bad, I can see the lessons, the things I needed to learn in order to be at the place I am now. They helped me grow, feel what I needed to feel, question my thoughts and actions and make different choices.

I can't tell you I believe in God in the traditional sense, but I do believe there is an energy, a universal life force that has created our world. I believe we are all connected in one way or another. That's my belief. What's your belief? Have you given it much thought lately? Are you a victim of circumstance, or is there a greater force working to give you life lessons so you can learn and grow into the best version of yourself? Are the obstacles in your way trying to teach you something? Are they there to slow you down and get you to think of an alternative that may be in your best interest?

What about a spiritual practice to help us heal physically and emotionally? Is it possible? In the movie *HEAL*, researcher and author Kelly Turner, Ph.D., talks about her research in the field of radical remissions and her studies of people from several different countries where she analyzed over 1,500 cases of different cancer types. Her research shows examples of how many people have healed from their disease—and not in the traditional way you might expect. Turner has identified over 75 different factors in their recoveries. Not everyone uses all 75 of these factors; however, when she looked at the data, all of these patients, now in remission, were using a common nine factors to help them recover. Only two were physical. The rest of these nine factors were based on mental, emotional and spiritual approaches. These factors are:

1. Radically changing your diet
2. Taking control of your health
3. Following your intuition
4. Using herbs and supplements
5. Releasing suppressed emotions
6. Increasing positive emotions
7. Embracing social support
8. Deepening your spiritual connection
9. Having a strong reason for living

She concluded that there really is a way to activate your immune system that goes beyond conventional wisdom. Much of it is grounded in spirituality and surrendering our trust to a higher intelligence or power that can accomplish anything, even when we can't foresee the outcome of a situation. Our spiritual path could be thought of as the ability to learn to let go and not try to control everything.

"When something moves you emotionally, trust and know you're on the right path. This emotion— whether anger, sadness, happiness or fear—holds important information for you to explore."
— Christine Porter

Whatever you believe is guiding you, be it God, Buddha, magic or love, it doesn't matter. When you believe you are a part of something larger than yourself, that what you are doing is a part of a greater purpose, you can begin to develop a faith in yourself. Maybe then you can begin to believe and trust you are living a purposeful life. Maybe all these life events you've experienced aren't just coincidences, but something larger than you guiding you down your true path. Something bigger than yourself is asking you to open your mind to new possibilities, to new viewpoints, to explore your life and learn from the lessons you are being given. This is the point where the struggle begins to lessen, the fear begins to ease and you can begin to view your life as more of an observer. You can ask the big questions: What am I here to learn from this experience? What am I being called to do? What do I believe in? How will I show up for my life fully?

30-Day Spirituality Challenge:

1. What are your beliefs? How do you see your world? Is your ego telling you it's a dangerous and scary place? Can you find examples of the goodness in the world around you and focus on those today?

2. Take out your journal and write down the most important life events that have happened to you. What did those life events teach you about your world? Were those situations planned or unexpected? How did you react? What new path did they lead you down? How have they influenced the decisions you make today?

3. Explore how you can contribute to your community or be more present with your family and kids. Is there a charity that touches your heart where you can volunteer or donate regularly? Is there a neighbor that may need a helping hand? Whatever little thing you can do has a ripple effect.

4. When you are tempted to judge other human beings, no matter how much you think they deserve it, remind yourself that everyone is doing the best they can from their own level of consciousness. This will help you feel more connected to others and the universe as a whole.

5. Embrace the unknown. When you begin to feel a new impulse, an uplifting thought, or an insight you have never thought of before, embrace this unknown.

Chapter 16:
Your Inside Job

As I conclude this book, I am feeling a sense of excitement to share my story and the practices and techniques that have transformed my life so dramatically. I am learning how to navigate change and let go of a lot of the stress and fear that was causing me so much pain and discomfort.

When I was struggling to find my way out of my own personal hell, I was searching for quick fixes. Another vacation, a new dress, more dinners out with friends, the next big discussion where my husband and I would make promises we could never keep. When I realized I just couldn't force my way out of my problems anymore, that's when I decided to sit still. It was a form of letting go of the resistance and the constant struggle to fix everything immediately. As a recovering worrier, letting go of the false sense of control and the chronic overthinking was a huge internal struggle. I always prided myself on having a solution for every problem. But a lot of times I made knee-jerk reactions so the problem would disappear quickly and I could move on. What I had thought were little problems and nuisances were really mini wakeup calls to get me to pay attention. When I didn't wake up, everything blew up.

When asked how was I feeling at the time, I often explained that I felt like I was living in a snow globe where someone would come along periodically and shake it up. I would visualize myself bobbing back and forth, trying to keep my footing so as to not fall over. I was allowing myself to be held hostage by other people's emotions and actions. If they were upset, I was upset. If there was a problem, it was my problem. I always jumped in to fix it. I had an over-exaggerated sense of responsibility with a little bit of "I know what's best" thrown in for good measure. I knew I was losing my footing, that I was spinning out of control, desperately clinging to any false sense of stability. That kept me in a job and a culture that was only making me feel worse about myself and the people around me. I was starting to feel like I was starring in my own bad reality show and I began acting just as terribly as the TV characters. I was caught up in the day-to-day drama.

The turmoil at home created the perfect storm. My resilience was wearing down as I tried to keep my dream going. Those were difficult times. I desperately clung to anything that would make me feel as if I had control. But I barely had control of myself.

There were plenty of well-meaning people who counseled me. I was told to try and forget about my pain and move on. Maybe I should take up writing, go for acupuncture to clear my energy, sage myself and my house, get more massages, get a new pet, join a group and find some new friends, try a drum circle, see a psychic to get clarity, watch more comedies, don't think so much, don't take life so seriously, just be happy, start dating, don't date, go on vacation, take a retreat, go to a sweat lodge, join a gym, take up Zumba, try past life regression therapy, clear my chakras, do more yoga. Just don't think about it anymore, and be happy. I tried many of these, no matter how silly some of them seemed. I was ready to try anything. Some provided short-term relief. But they didn't get to the core of the problem. I was lost. And in a lot of pain.

I knew I had to take a leap of faith, to trust something other than my controlling mind. I didn't want to just shut down or forget about what had happened over the past five years. I wanted to sit with it, examine it, figure out how my best thinking had got me to this place of crisis. I didn't ever want to feel this deep, almost unimaginable pain again, so this was it: I was going to feel everything, no numbing myself with food, alcohol, or too much television or going out on the town. I was going to try and sift through and sort out all the messiness of my life.

At the core of it, I had to let go. In the weeks and months after my big life crisis, leaving my marriage and my job, I felt the emotional heaviness I had been carrying begin to lift. I found meditating and practicing mindfulness was a way for me to begin to let go of my old patterns and create a new life for myself. The quiet introspection was surprisingly comforting. I developed a deeper connection with myself. I learned I was more fragile in some areas and stronger in others, and that was okay. I paid attention to the internal dialogue that was playing in my head and began to see how I was creating great anxiety in my life with my habitual thought patterns. I became brave enough to explore my hopes and dreams without judgement.

Journaling provided the self-expression and self-reflection I needed to help me sort out my feelings. Practicing gratitude for what I had and not focusing on the loss, developing my spirituality, taking care of myself and eating well were all important in creating a life with less fear and more confidence.

I hope you find the life of your dreams and you never forget that everything you need is right inside of you. Your intuitive sense, your heart's purpose, it's all there trying to get your attention. The transformation begins when you tap into that inner voice that knows exactly what you need. It has been there all along waiting for you to sit still and listen. That is the beautiful wisdom of you.

Acknowledgments

There are so many incredible people who have helped me along the way to fulfilling my dream. My dear friend Tracy for being my cheerleader, my visionary and my right hand in this wonderful and sometimes chaotic journey. You are my dear friend and I love you for always being by my side. A huge hug to Jennifer who has also been by my side cheering me on and providing wisdom and support. My mother who was a huge force in me writing this book. She always believed in me even when I didn't believe in myself. A big thank you to Cathy and Marguerite for your encouragement and support. And a special thank you to all the people I've had the privilege to support in my workshops, retreats and online. You are the reason I continue this journey as a Soulful Warrior. I hope you find this book inspiring and you feel the big hug I'm giving you as you explore the wisdom of you. You are powerful, you are strong and you are the change leaders that the world needs most right now!

About the author

CHRISTINE PORTER is an author, coach, speaker, doggie mom and yogi. She is also the creative founder of the international company, Peace and Pear, LLC, a mindfulness company creating products that feed your soul. A self-proclaimed Soulful Warrior, she is committed to helping people create an extraordinary life and go from surviving to thriving. Porter's workshops, retreats, products and books all focus on helping people connect with their inner wisdom to alleviate pain and stress and to find their power, passion and purpose. A graduate of

Michigan State University, her post graduate work was with the Institute for Integrative Nutrition where she received her board certification as a Health and Wellness Coach. She is also the author of Healthy, Sexy and Fit™, a 21-day kick start program for increasing energy, weight loss and a healthier mind and body. Christine lives with her favorite pooch, Bodhi in Upstate New York.

For more on Christine's work, visit www.PeaceandPear.com and follow her on Facebook at: Facebook.com/PeaceandPear and on Instagram under the user name: @PeaceandPear. Christine is available for select workshops, book readings and other speaking engagements throughout the United States. To inquire about bookings or coaching, please contact her directly at Christine@PeaceandPear.com

A LIFE COACH IN A BOX.

You want and need something but can't quite place your finger on it. You often lose sight of what it is you need or want because the noise of day-to-day life seems so loud.

Soulful Connections is a 120- card deck of thought-provoking questions created to guide you down a path of self-discovery and find your passion and purpose.

The questions are powerful in their simplicity. Some are creative: *What makes you unique?* Some are self reflective; *Where do you want to be a year from now?* and *What is your greatest fear and has it come true?* Others are whimsical and fun but can provide great insight; *If your life was a movie, what would the title be?*

To learn more and see all the ways people are using Soulful Connections, visit us at

www.PeaceandPear.com.

Made in the USA
Lexington, KY
30 October 2019

56152279R00102